Unsung Heroes

Eastbourne's Fire Service
1824 - 1974

Stephen le Vine

Front cover image by Marco Allasio
Rear cover image. Old fire appliance on display at Whitley Road fire station.
Damian Stoneham.

First Published 2021
Published by Loncastle South
5/19, Upper Avenue, Eastbourne,
East Sussex. BN21 3XR U.K.
e-mail: loncastlesouth@yahoo.co.uk

British Library Cataloguing in Publication Data.
A catalogue record for this book is available from the British Library.
ISBN: 0993544132   ISBN-13: 978-0-9935441-3-2

DEDICATION

To all the brave firemen and women both past and present who unselfishly serve the community. They daily risk their lives to save others both day and night.

Memorial on display at Whitley Road Fire Station.

I am indebted to Kevin Gordon for agreeing to write a foreword for my book. Kevin is a retired British Transport Police officer and 'Chronicler' at Seaford museum. He is an Honorary Historian for Seaford Town Council and a committee member of the Eastbourne History Society. Kevin has written several books on the history of Eastbourne and Seaford.

S.L.   *April 2021*

FOREWORD

I distinctly remember watching the dark smoke billowing from the fire on the pier in 1971. A few days later I entered the blackened shell of the pier buildings and witnessed at first hand the acrid smelling monochrome remains of a once splendid seaside theatre. Firemen were still there amongst the still-smoking remains. The Fire Brigade are an essential service.

The history of a town's Fire Brigade can be relatively simple, but this is not the case at Eastbourne as there are a number of features that make the town unique. Thanks to the patronage of the Duke of Devonshire, it became one of the country's leading seaside resorts, its hotels crammed with tens of thousands of visitors, surrounded by downland which, during the summer months can easily catch fire. And during the dark days of the Second World War, it became a target for Luftwaffe bombing raids. There have even been fires on passing ships that have needed to be dealt with. In Eastbourne therefore the history of the town is intertwined with the history of its fire brigade.

This book tells the story of the brave men who sought to keep Eastbourne safe. Stephen leVine documents the early days of firefighting in the town when, remarkably, there were two rival brigades. As the town developed so did its fire-fighting capabilities, and Stephen carefully lists the increasingly complex equipment provided from the early hand-pumps to the huge fully-equipped fire tenders with escape-ladders.

The town was and still is proud of its fire-service, and this book is not just a list of fires but also reveals the human aspects of the service, with regular drills, displays, dinners, dances and prize-giving. I particularly liked the huge commemorative arches set up when royalty graced our town.

I am pleased that Stephen's meticulous research has filled a gap in the story of Eastbourne with this well-illustrated and comprehensive book.

Motcombe, March 2021   Kevin Gordon

ESRO

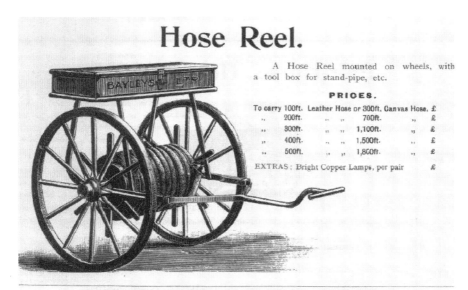

Hose Reel.

A Hose Reel mounted on wheels, with a tool box for stand-pipe, etc.

PRICES.

To carry 100ft.	Leather Hose or	300ft.	Canvas Hose.	£		
,,	200ft.	,, ,,	700ft.		,,	£
,,	300ft.	,, ,,	1,100ft.		,,	£
,,	400ft.	,, ,,	1,500ft.		,,	£
,,	500ft.	,, ,,	1,800ft.		,,	£

EXTRAS : Bright Copper Lamps, per pair   £

FIRE ESCAPE WORKS, SOUTHWARK, LONDON.

CONTENTS

	Foreword	iv
	Acknowledgements	viii
1	Introduction	1
2	Early Years	7
3	County Borough of Eastbourne	25
4	New Century	43
5	Reorganisation	73
6	War Years	89
7	Returned Fire Appliances	105
8	E/B Borough Fire Brigade	107
9	Fire Stations	143
10	Recreation	153
11	Equipment	157
12	Chief Officers	173
13	Some Major Incidents	175
14	Last Word	187
15	Bibliography	189

Merryweather 60ft Ladder Escape

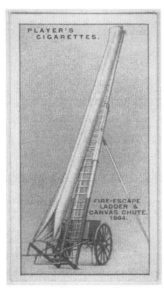

Merryweather

Bayley's Escape Ladder

Fig 46—MERRYWEATHER'S HAND FIRE ESCAPE

ACKNOWLEDGMENTS

I would like to sincerely thank the many people who have helped me in my research for this publication. I would particularly like to thank the East Sussex Records Office (ESRO), Heritage Eastbourne, The National Archives and The British Newspaper Archive. Also, the many ex-firemen and their relatives for their valuable assistance and their help with my book. Photographs from private collections were generously donated and where possible I have acknowledged the source. Special thanks to Guy Bowes, Aidan Fisher, Colin Fox, Robert Francis, Dave Freeman, Michael Garrett, Richard Goldsmith, Bruce Hoad, Rosalind Hodges, David Holt, Roger C. Mardon, Robert Sumsion, Pat Smith, Damian Stoneham, and Peter Winter MBE. I am especially indebted to Simon Williams for his knowledge, patience and guidance with editing my book. Kevin Gordon, a local historian and an author, kindly agreed to write the foreword to the book, for which I am sincerely grateful.

Disclaimer:

Time line

Fire Engines.

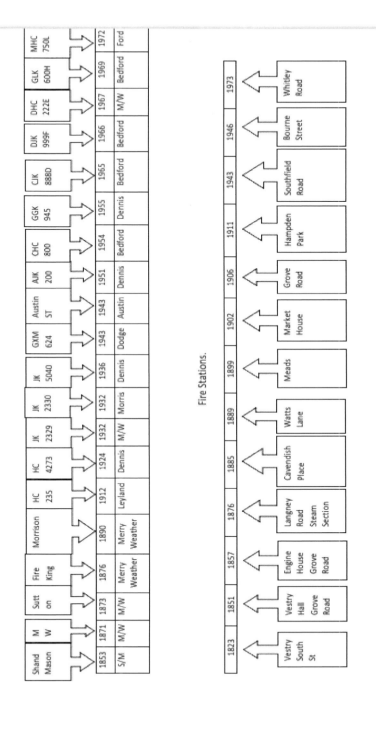

Shand Mason	MW	Sutton	Fire King	Morrison	HC 235	HC 4273	JK 2329	JK 2330	JK 5040	GXM 624	Austin ST	AJK 200	CHC 800	GGK 945	CJK 888D	DJK 999F	DHC 222E	GLK 600H	MHC 750L
1853	1871	1873	1876	1890	1912	1924	1932	1932	1936	1943	1943	1951	1954	1955	1965	1966	1967	1969	1972
S/M	M/W	M/W	Merry Weather	Merry Weather	Leyland	Dennis	M/W	Morris	Dennis	Dodge	Austin	Dennis	Bedford	Dennis	Bedford	Bedford	M/W	Bedford	Ford

Fire Stations.

1823	1851	1857	1876	1885	1889	1899	1902	1906	1911	1943	1946	1973
Vestry South St	Vestry Hall Grove Road	Engine House Grove Road	Langney Road Steam Section	Cavendish Place	Watts Lane	Meads	Market House	Grove Road	Hampden Park	Southfield Road	Bourne Street	Whitley Road

1824 First water pump + 1932 Morris turntable ladder appliance.

1933 Dennis appliance

1 INTRODUCTION

Humans first discovered how to make fire back in the Palaeolithic period. And since that time, they have fought how to use and control this destructive force that they have unleashed. There have always been wildfires. These can occur naturally and in some countries are the most common form of natural disaster. We live on a planet with seasonal high temperatures and dry periods and an Earth covered in carbon-rich vegetation. This, together with our oxygen atmosphere. With frequent volcanic occurrences, and regular lightning storms have caused many destructive fires over the centuries.

There is evidence that there were firefighting teams in operation in Alexandria, Egypt. When an engineer named Ctesibius invented the first force pump (c250 BC). We also know that a firefighting force used water pumps in Ancient Rome. Marcus Licinius Crassus (c.115 BC or 112 BC–53 BC) formed the first Roman fire brigade with 500 firefighters. He was a General and politician and became one of the richest men in Rome. Later Caesar Augustus in AD 6 formed the Vigiles Urbani (watchmen of the city). This was initially made up of slaves to fight fires in the city. They organised these men into seven cohorts of Watchmen. Each cohort composed of 1000 men known as 'vigilanti'. They stationed these men around the city, but they only had leather buckets and hooks to deal with fires. Wealthy inhabitants of the city had night watchmen in their houses to warn of any fires occurring. During this period, they have estimated that Rome had two million inhabitants. We generally believe that the first organised firefighting force in Britain was during the Roman invasion. This was in AD 43. They only used simple pumps and leather buckets of water to douse the flames together with rudimentary water siphons. After the Romans left, it took many years before there were firefighting teams in the country.

In 1285 Edward 1 passed an Act ordering every city and town to appoint a night watchman. The crime of arson was considered high treason.

As urban living became more popular, the risks of fire were greater, especially as medieval towns were constructed with wood. The buildings had thatched roofs, with the risk of fire a constant worry for the citizens.

The town's Watchman, and then the Vestry (The Vestry, a committee of local secular and clerical inhabitants who governed the parish) arranged fire protection for the population. Later, the parish councils took on the responsibility of fighting fires. There were no regulations or standards in place. It was not until much later that it became law for local officials to supply an organised firefighting force and protect the townsfolk and their property.

There were only basic hand-operated fire pumps available to fight fires at this time.

It was in 1625 that Roger James invented the first British patented fire pump. The following year Exeter received a two-man manual pump equipped with four leather buckets, two horn lanterns, a glass lantern and a Watchman's rattle. It was in use a hundred years later. They reported in 1903 that the appliance was still in working order.

A Dutchman, Jan Van der Heides is credited with inventing the modern hosepipe. Initially, he made them with sailcloth cut in long strips and sewn together. Later, he used fifty-foot hand-stitched leather strips with brass couplings. These helped firefighters to position themselves closer to the fires. Richard Newsham of London made a much-improved engine design in 1721. This engine could throw out or empty one hundred and ten gallons of water in one minute. In 1725 Newsham patented another improved fire engine when he introduced an engine with side operating handles and foot treadles.

There was no organised firefighting service in London before the Great Fire of 1666. At the time they estimated the cost of the fire to the City of London at ten million pounds. With the destruction of over 13,000 houses and the displacement of about 100,000 people. The fire raged in the city for four days. This tragedy prompted insurance companies to form private fire brigades. The insurance companies issued the first Fire Insurance Policies in London in 1667. Dr Nicholas Barbon, an insurance pioneer in 1680, created the first brigade. He recruited men who were mainly watermen and provided their uniforms. They also issued the crews with large gilt or silver badges. They wore these high up on the left arm of the men and bore the company's insignia.

Insurance brigades would try to only fight fires in those buildings their company insured. To identify these, they placed a fire insurance mark on the outside of the building. The marks were metal plaques with the company's emblem embossed on them. In 1680, the insurance company 'The Fire Office' was the first to issue these. Their emblem was a Phoenix rising from the flames. These brigades primary concern was the saving of the property.

If the building they attended was not insured by them, then they would seek to recover costs from the insuring company of the building.

The last insurance brigade operating was the Norwich Union in Worcester, who disbanded in 1929.

According to historic records, the first municipal fire brigade in Europe was the Pompier Corps of Paris. They formed this in 1716 although records show that in 1699 fire engines were first used in the city. They called these 'Pompes Portatives'. In Berlin in 1851, then the capital of Prussia, they created the Berlin Fire Brigade. Although the first known fire engine in Germany was recorded in 1615.

The first municipal fire brigade in Britain was in 1824, after the Great Fire of Edinburgh. They named it the Edinburgh Police Fire Engine Establishment and Fire Master James Braidwood led this service. Six insurance companies and the City jointly funded this. A few years later, in 1830, Mr Braidwood published a firefighting training manual. This was the *On the Construction of Fire Engines and Apparatus, the Training of Firemen, and the Method of Proceeding in Cases of Fire.* In

James Braidwood

1833 he moved to London as the first Fire Chief of the recently formed London Fire Engine Establishment (LFEE). This was a consortium of ten independent insurance companies. The service had eighty men and nineteen fire stations throughout the city. In 1861 on the 22 June, James Braidwood whilst attending a warehouse fire in Tooley Street, London, died when a wall fell on him. He was buried in London and it is reported that his funeral cortège was one and a half miles long.

Mr John Hudson formed the Fire Escape Society in 1828, and private donations funded the society. But they soon founded and were later absorbed by the Royal Society for the Protection of Life from Fire (RSPLF). The Society provided six-wheeled escape ladders in the larger towns. This helped to rescue people and aided escape from tall burning buildings. They usually kept the ladders in churchyards during the day and placed them on street corners at night. They had special wheeled escape ladders that could reach up to 60ft high, and many fire brigades around the country used this type of ladder right up to 1984. The RSPLF now exists to give recognition to anyone who performs acts of bravery in rescuing others from fire.

So, when was the first Eastbourne Fire Service formed?

The earliest form of firefighting equipment recorded in Eastbourne is in 1824, when the Vestry purchased a manual pump.

They arranged for groups of volunteer men to operate the machine and to travel to and fight fires. At this time there were three firefighting machines available in the town. One at the Vestry and another at the Compton Place Estates, the military barracks also had firefighting equipment. With the reforms of the government in 1859, they set up the Local Board and formed a Volunteer Fire Brigade. After a short while, the Board procured the Vestry manual engine.

The first appliances were hand carts and these carried hoses and buckets, with water coming from nearby ponds. Later they introduced horse-drawn hand pumps, these could connect hoses using a standpipe to local hydrants or ponds. Steam engines were a significant advance, even though it could take ten minutes for them to stoke the fire and be ready to extinguish the blaze. They would usually use two horses to pull the engines, but if they called the brigade to attend to a fire some distance away, they would hitch up another pair of horses. The coming of motor engines and water tenders aided the fight against fires. Crews now could dispatch the appliances in minutes and did not have to wait to find horses. They were dousing the flames immediately on arrival at the scene.

After more changes in local government, Eastbourne became a Borough in 1884. They formed the new Eastbourne County Borough Fire Brigade. With the threat of war, the Fire Brigade Act 1938 came into force. This saw the creation of the Auxiliary Fire Service, followed by the National Fire Service in 1941. The national government would now provide all services.

At the end of WW2, the government returned control of the fire service to local councils, and the Borough renamed the service the Borough of Eastbourne Fire Brigade (1948). There were more changes in 1974, and the Borough fire service now came under the name of the East Sussex Fire Brigade. On the first of April 1997, and because of further local government reorganisation, they renamed the service again. We now know them as the East Sussex Fire & Rescue Service, covering all East Sussex and the city of Brighton and Hove, which has a separate unitary local government but is ceremonially within the county of East Sussex. Their headquarters are in Lewes, and Eastbourne fire station is now a training and community fire station.

Times change and local government throughout the country have now lost control of the organisation and running of its fire services. Fire personnel are now more professionally trained, with colleges set up to educate firefighters in the art of dealing with fires. Eastbourne was in control of its firefighting service from the past days of the Vestry, then the Local Board and the Borough of Eastbourne. But since 1974 Eastbourne local government has lost authority over its fire service.

****

Robert Sumsion

Unknown date of early photo with Captain J Hounsom in the centre.

1876 Merryweather   *ESRO*

1895/8 At Cavendish Place   *Colin Fox*

1899 Grove Road   *ESRO*

2 EARLY YEARS

The town of Eastbourne came about with the joining of three hamlets, known as South Bourne, Meads, and Sea Houses. Later this included East Bourne (Old Town), situated a little inland. Until the early 1700s, the residents composed of landowners, farmers and fisherman. Their hamlets were quite isolated. The settlements by the sea developed with the coming of the railway in May 1849, and Eastbourne prospered when they built a new rail branch line to Polegate. It joined the town to London, Brighton and the South Coast railway system. William Cavendish, the 7th Duke of Devonshire, the largest landowner in 1859, requested Henry Currey, the Duke's agent, to design and layout plans for a new town. A town "for gentlemen by gentlemen". Then development and expansion in the town started.

Residents tackled fires using buckets and water from nearby ponds. In past years, these often occurred in houses or on farmland. Arson caused many of the fires on the farms, an occurrence that happened in many other counties throughout England. It was common knowledge that gangs of disgruntled workers travelled around the country setting fires. In Sussex, the 1830s was a particularly riotous time with many fires reported. With the governance of the town in the hands of the Vestry, they organised groups of volunteers to fight fires. But they only had rudimentary firefighting equipment.

There had been a military barracks in Eastbourne since 1794. And a report from the *Sussex Advertiser* in June 1811 mentions a fire on a farm where nearly £1,000 of damage occurred. It took over twenty-four hours for the men to extinguish the blaze. There is no mention of firefighters from Eastbourne attending, but the *Sussex Advertiser* reports that Lieut. Gordon, Commander of the Ordnance Department, dispatched their fire engine to help. There was another report later of a fire near the church. When again the local barracks supplied their firefighting equipment.

Earlier, on 3rd June as reported in the *Sussex Advertiser,* and during a terrific storm, lightning hit a large barn owned by Charles Gilbert. The Artillery barracks sent their fire engine. It took many hours before they extinguished the blaze and the farm sustained almost £2,000 of damage.

There had been a report in the newspaper of February 1831 of arson. This was on the farm of Mr Moses Filder, a tenant of Lord Cavendish.

There is no mention of firefighters from Eastbourne attending but reports that Lieut. Gordon, Commander of the Ordnance Department, sent their fire engine to help. The estimated damage at this fire was between £700 and £1,000.

This is not the first arson attack on Mr Filder's farm. There was an incident on his farm a few months earlier. And back in 1805, he and his family escaped a similar occurrence when a fire destroyed his house and barn. Mr Filder offered a reward of £100 to find the offender. A short while later they apprehended a 15-year-old boy. At a fire in the following January, also on a farm, both the Parish engine and Board of Ordinance engine attended.

The Vestry office was in South Street, next to the Police Station, and they held rudimentary fire equipment. According to Vestry minutes, the earliest known Manual fire pump in the town was purchased in 1824. This was the same year as the formation of the first municipal fire brigade in Britain. (They called the new brigade, the Edinburgh Fire Engine Establishment). The new appliance was probably a fire pump manufactured by Richard Newsham or by Messrs Braithwaite & Ericsson of New Road, London. Newsham later built the first steam fire engines in Britain. Firefighters used this type of appliance in London.

Although many towns and villages had a volunteer fire service it was the passing of the Watching and Lighting Act 1835 applying to parishes that it became a legal requirement for them to offer a fire service. They would have to arrange "Sergeants of the Night, Watchmen, Patrols" and, "The said inspectors shall provide and keep up Fire Engines, with Pipes and other Utensils proper for same…". The Towns Police Act of 1847 allowed towns/village councils to buy firefighting appliances and the authority to set up their own fire stations. They could charge the payment of fire crews and equipment against the Poor Rates.

Eastbourne, by the 1840s, had two firefighting appliances. One Manual pump owned by the Parish and another Manual on the Compton Place Estate. The one in Compton Place, built by Hadley, Simpkin and Lott about the 1820s, was not maintained and deteriorated. They found it years later in pieces in the Towner Art Gallery basement. Volunteers recovered the appliance, and with some replacements rebuilt the machine. This is now on display in the Whitley Road fire station. The original Manual pump owned by the Parish was found in the cellar of Grove Road station in the 1930s and later renovated. They kept it at the fire station on display. Unfortunately, with the bombing of the Grove Road fire station in 1943, the pump was destroyed.

The Parish pump was not being regularly maintained. When there was a fire on a farm off South Street on 5 November 1847, the Compton Place and Ordinance Yard appliances attended. At the next Parish meeting, after this fire, they brought up the condition of the Parish fire engine. They asked members to guarantee payment for urgent repairs that the engine needed. This they all agreed to do.

After local businessman, John Haine sponsored the construction of a new building in 1851, the Vestry and the Manual pump moved into the premises in Grove Road.

Their new hall had cost £270 to build, and in July 1896 became the library. Later in 1902, they demolished this building to make way for the Technical Institute.

January 1853 saw a fire in the Grey's Mansion owned by D. J. Gilbert. The Compton Place and Ordinance fire appliances attended. They discovered the fire at 3.30 on Saturday afternoon of the 15th. For three and a half hours, they fought the blaze until they finally brought it under control. They reported that the adjoining house owned by Mr Henry Bradford had sustained substantial damage.

The Parish pump needed repair, as it was often proving difficult to use. So, after receiving many complaints from residents, at a Vestry meeting in February, they formed a committee. This was to examine the condition of the engine and find out the cost of repairs. Later in the month, they received a quotation from Messrs Warner & Co in London for fifty pounds for the work. This covered repairs and the supply of 120ft of new hose and brackets. The company suggested that as the engine was old, they would carry out the repair but informed the council that these repairs would not last long.

They advised they could supply a new and more powerful engine complete with hoses and brackets for £140. The authorities then decided that with the financial help of local businesses, residents and donations from insurance offices they could buy more modern equipment. They collectively raised £150 for a new fire engine.

In July, the Committee purchased a Shand Mason fire engine. They arranged for it to be dispatched from London by train. And it arrived complete with hoses, buckets and extra equipment. The new engine would now come under the authority of an inspector appointed under the Watching and Lighting Act. They then took the fire engine out for a public display. This was to reassure citizens and to show the new fire capabilities to the residents of the town.

Although the town had enough volunteers available to fight fires, the Committee noted there wasn't anyone in charge to organise the men. Also, they observed that the firemen were not properly maintaining their equipment. So, following the Watching and Lighting Act, in November they formed a Volunteer Fire Brigade. They appointed Mr William Simpson as Superintendent.

ESRO

With the present arrangement, they found it difficult to house the new fire engine at the Vestry, so they decided that they required a new building. In July 1857 they constructed the first purpose-built fire station in Eastbourne. This cost eighty pounds and they named it the Parish Engine House. The building was near the Vestry Hall in Grove Road and roughly opposite the entrance to Ivy Terrace.

Following the Local Government Act 1858, they formed the Local Government Board (1859–1883) and elected Reginald J. Graham as their first chairman. In Eastbourne, as in other places, the Board took over most civic duties from the Vestry Committees and held their first meeting in the Vestry Hall on 14 January 1859. The Vestry still had some control until the Local Government Act 1894, and the formation of Parish Councils.

At the Vestry meeting in April 1859, the Lighting Committee report recommended that they should buy more hoses, a pair of shafts, and a set of single harnesses. They also suggested that they should increase Superintendent William Simpson's pay from four pounds to five pounds. The fire engine should have quarterly inspections, and the brigade should exercise regularly. For the men attending the drill, "we should pay them 2s 6d each for every drill practice". The Committee agreed, and they passed the motion, although the matter was still a point of discussion at the meeting in October.

The Borough Surveyor produced a report again requesting extra hoses and a pair of shafts. He suggested ten men should be in the brigade, and the pay should be 5s per drill. Then he recommended that they should buy an escape ladder. The Committee agreed to pay 2s 6d per man who attended drills, and they deferred the matter of a fire escape.

The Lighting Committee met on Monday 1 December 1862 and agreed that they required extra hoses. Together with ladders for the town fire engine and they passed the motion. They were still discussing the question about a fire escape. This matter took many more years to resolve. It was customary for each firefighter to carry a key to turn on the water from the hydrants. If there was a delay in the Captain/Superintendent arriving at the scene of the fire, the men could start fighting the fire immediately.

The population of the four hamlets that made up Eastbourne at this time was about 3,800 persons. The Shand Mason appliance and the old 1823 machine was owned by the Vestry with the Local Board responsible for the administration of the fire service. The Local Board meeting in June 1865 confirmed that the accounts for the previous year for the Fire Engine account amounted to £26 13s 9d.

When the Lighting Committee met the following May they agreed to buy a hose reel costing £11 10s. They also tested the fire engine and found it to be in perfect working order.

At last, in 1867, the Board purchased a new fire escape ladder. In July they brought out the new Merryweather's escape ladder on which the brigade could practice. The firemen ran the ladder, which they kept by Trinity Church, along the streets and up to the Diplock Lion Brewery in Pevensey Road. The council then decided that the firemen should practice regularly with the ladder.

It was reported in the *Sussex Advertiser* newspaper in August, that the Local Board had set up the Eastbourne Volunteer Fire Brigade. This was only for administration, and not financial support and the Board appointed Charles Tomes as captain. He had overall charge of the new brigade. Mr Tomes was the Local Board's surveyor, and it was on his suggestion that the Board set up the new fire service.

Twenty-five persons had come forward to join the brigade and were selected as members. They took the Parish fire engine out for a practice and to test the efficiency of the engine. First, they went to Hartington Place and onto Devonshire Place. To fund the service, they made a collection. This was from local businesses and individuals. The money helped to pay a small allowance to the volunteers for attending fires and fund the purchase of uniforms and other equipment that they required.

In these early years, the brigade had "call-boys". They did not yet have telephone communications to the firemen. When a fire was notified to the fire station, these young volunteers would run around the town and would knock on each house alerting the firemen to the fire. The men would then make their way either to the fire or the fire station. Many of these volunteers later joined the brigade as firefighters. One of these young boys, George Terry, joined when he was 14 years old. Sixty years later he was still serving in the brigade answering calls to duty. He was not attending fires but remained in the station house to answer the telephone and attend to other duties.

One of the first fire call outs for the new brigade was for a member of the brigade, Mr Lucken. He was a draper with a shop in Seaside when on 29 August a fire broke out. With the help from passing volunteers and the arrival of the fire engine, they extinguished the blaze within twenty minutes.

In these early days, the cause of most fires was from dripping candles, blocked chimneys or accidental spillage in the home/business. The firemen could control them using buckets and a fire hose connected to nearby hydrants.

With the new brigade, the Local Board arranged at Christmas to proceed through the town and display their engines and equipment to the townspeople. The men were in full uniform, red coats and brass helmets. The fire engine and escape ladder started at the Gilbert Arms. The procession continued through to Southbourne, along the Grand Parade and up to Meads. All twenty-eight members of the brigade took part in the procession. The volunteer firefighters all came from a mix of local businesses with Mr Tomes, a surveyor. Others were builders, a blacksmith, carpenters, labourers and shop owners.

The accounts for the year 1867 showed subscriptions from members of the public and business companies, together with a fund-raising concert, amounted to £35 12s. Expenses for hiring the horses from Mr Greenfield, costs to Merryweather for equipment, and sundries amounted to £34 11s. This left a surplus of £1 1s for the year. By the next half-yearly meeting in July 1868, matters had deteriorated. The accounts showed a shortfall of £64 10s due mainly to uncollected promises. By May 1870, the *Eastbourne Gazette* reported that the Volunteer Fire Brigade was lacking funds and could be disbanded. They suggested that the Local Board "if it has the power, take the brigade under its sheltering wings".

Given disagreements with other members about the running of the service, Mr Tomes resigned in April 1871 from the fire brigade. The members held a meeting and appointed Mr Henry Brown as their new Captain.

They appointed Mr T. H. Headland as Treasurer of the Brigade. In a letter to the Board, Mr Brown stated he was happy to take up the position of Captain, but wished to have complete control of the brigade's appliances.

The members informed Mr Brown that the firemen were not prepared to use the fire escape because of its dangerous condition. It needed urgent repair. They advised him that the Lighting Committee were in control of the Fire Brigade and the firefighting equipment. They adjourned the matter until the next meeting of the Board.

To raise funds and awareness, the brigade held a parade and then a dance at the Assembly Rooms in October. The fire engine from the Engine House together with the one from Compton Place and the one from the Artillery paraded through the town. This was also a chance for the brigade to show off their new uniforms. A dark blue jacket, unlike their earlier bright red ones. They stopped at various places en route and put on a re-enactment and demonstration of the engines and escape ladder for the residents. After travelling to a different part of the town, they repeated their display before attending a concert in the evening.

The brigade was independent of the Local Board and they did not have control over the fire engine and fire escape ladder. As the Captain was in charge of all the equipment and its use, the Board requested the brigade should hand over the appliances to them. This they agreed to.

Then the Board discovered the fire engine and escape ladder needed repair. They contacted Messrs Merryweather for a quote for the repairs.

After they received this, the Lighting and Building Committee agreed they needed a new appliance.

The *Eastbourne Gazette* on 29 November published an announcement by the fire brigade. This advised that in their opinion the protection of the town was not adequate against fire. Especially regarding the taller buildings in town. The Parish engine could only throw a jet of water thirty feet, just enough for ordinary dwellings. Should any fire occur in larger structures such as in Grand Parade, then the brigade would have to request aid from Hastings or Lewes. This would take time and the fire would have a greater hold on the building.

The number of members in the fire service was now thirty, and they agreed that the cost of a new engine would be £140. But the Local Board was unwilling to pay this. So, Mr Fuller suggested that they would put the matter in the hands of trustees on behalf of the town, with subscriptions made to the 'Engine Fund'.

At long last, the brigade bought a new fire engine from Messrs Merryweather & Co, who delivered it by train in December.

The Board elected Mr Towner, Captain of the Volunteer Brigade's Manual Section, and Mr Thomas Fuller as Captain of the Steam Section.

At the annual meeting of the brigade in January 1872, they reported that the number of fires attended was 112. This was considerably higher than in the past and 31 more incidents than in the previous year. Also, most of the fires attended during the year were not of a serious matter and were dealt with by the use of their hoses. They advised that the subscriptions, donations and proceeds received from the Swiss Gardens' Fete amounted to £106 7s 7d, leaving a balance for the year of £2 11s 5d.

They needed to store the new engine undercover, and the brigade had problems of where to keep it. At first, they requested to put in the Parish Engine House. But that created a fuss with members of the Vestry who complained. In their meeting in March, they said that the engine was private property. And it was not right for the parish to house the appliance in the Parish Engine House. The fact was, the Local Board had refused to buy this machine.

The brigade had bought it and passed the engine over to a trust for the benefit of the town. So, for the next three months, they housed the new engine at Mr C. Bradford's Royal Victoria Mews livery stables. The brigade was thankful as he did not charge them for the housing of the engine. This entire matter had been drawing on for months. Finally, in the April meeting of the Lighting and Building Committee, they agreed to let the fire brigade house their new Merryweather fire engine in the Parish Engine House.

In July, the brigade paid eighty pounds on account to Merryweather and Company for the new fire engine. The brigade then held a contest on the Cricket Ground to raise more funds. Mr J. C. Merryweather agreed to attend and present silver cups to winning participants. He would also send down to Eastbourne one of his latest steam engines. Eastbourne Fire Brigade invited seven brigades from Surrey and Sussex to take part in the competition. All the proceeds from the day, going to pay the balance still outstanding on the new engine. The engines assembled and then proceeded around the town before gathering at the Cricket Ground. Unfortunately, the weather was awful with heavy rain and with few spectators. The takings of the day only amounted to £35, not enough to pay off the outstanding amount due to Merryweather & Co.

Grand Volunteer
FIRE BRIGADE CONTEST
IN THE
EASTBOURNE CRICKET GROUND,
MONDAY, AUGUST, 5th.

Under the patronage of His Grace the Duke of Devonshire, K.G., Lord Edward Cavendish, and the Hon. Mrs. Gilbert.

SILVER CUPS and other PRIZES.

A HOUSE WILL BE SET ON FIRE.

THE USE OF THE FIRE ESCAPE
in rescuing life, and throwing water on roofs, &c.,
illustrated.

A powerful Steam Engine will be worked.
The prizes will be presented by Mrs. Jeffery.
Proceedings to commence at 2.30 p.m.
Judges:—Messrs. J. MERRYWEATHER and C. TOMES, and CAPT. HOLMAN.
Referee:—DR. JEFFERY.
Admission, Sixpence; Reserved Space, 6d. extra.
For further particulars see programme.
Tickets for reserved space may be obtained of the Hon. Sec., Mr. Fuller, Victoria Baths, 23, Grand Parade.

E/B Gazette 31July1872

They arranged another concert to raise funds for the new fire engine and held this on Monday 2 September at the Diplock's Assembly Room. Although a full evening's program was put on the attendance was small.

The brigade in 1873 bought a Steamer fire engine, and in 1880, in a ceremony at the town hall, they named the engine 'Sutton'. It was initially bought on credit whilst the brigade waited for the collection of contributions from the public and local business. The arrangement with Merryweather & Co was that the balance, £60, outstanding in February, was due by March. If not paid, they would have to return the engine, and the brigade would pay a hire charge for the engine. Captain Fuller and Engineer George Gausden stepped forward and guaranteed payment.

On the 10 November, there was the Great Volunteer Fire Brigade Demonstration. They held this at Crystal Palace in London. The Eastbourne Brigade with Captain Brown attended and competed against fifteen other teams from around the country. In the first competition for a four-man team, they won the first prize of ten pounds. Captain Brown was highly complimented for his Brigades efficiency and smartness.

Later in the month, James Towner replaced Henry Brown as Captain of the brigade. Mr Greenfield who supplied horses to the brigade resigned as the driver of the Parish engine in February 1874. He suggested that they get their horses from a different source. At this time the Parish had one appliance, and the Local Board had another.

Funds were not always forthcoming. In April they reported in the *Eastbourne Gazette* that income for the Volunteer Fire Brigade the previous year was £16 18s 9d. Unfortunately, the expenditure was £22 12s 9d.

Captain Towner was requesting subscriptions or donations from "any who may feel disposed to aid so noble a cause".

They held the annual fire drill trials and competitions at Crystal Palace in July where nineteen fire brigades from around the country took part. This included the Eastbourne Brigade. Over thirty fire engines were in attendance. And eight thousand spectators watched the day's activities. On this occasion, Eastbourne did not carry off any prizes.

At the Local Board meeting in October, there were calls for the fire brigade to obtain new hose connectors, as at a recent fire at Rodmill, it had taken the brigade fifteen to twenty minutes to connect their hoses to the fire engine.

They had four different fittings and enough hoses, but the threads were defective. They estimated the cost to be £71.

In the following November, at the Peerless timber yard, there was an enormous fire. The fire was first reported at 10 p.m. and caused over £5,000 of damage. The timber yard was situated at the west end of Langney Road, by the junction with Terminus Road. Yards and buildings had a frontage of two hundred feet to Langney Road with an entrance at the west end.

There were offices and a wheelwright's shop on the ground floor and carpenters' workrooms on the floor above them. Stables and a paint shop were nearby.

The Eastbourne Volunteer Fire Brigade (with horses still being supplied by Mr Greenfield) rushed to the scene of the blaze as soon as they received the alarm. The Royal Artillery also sent their manual fire appliances and arrived thirty minutes after the Volunteer Brigade. Men from the coastguard assisted the firemen with hoses trained upon the fire. Even the small manual fire appliance based at Compton Place rushed to assist fighting the fire. The firefighters finally extinguished the blaze after five hours and there was minor damage to neighbouring premises. The brigade was still in attendance the following day, putting out small patches of fire that persisted.

This was one of the largest fires that Eastbourne had seen and could be viewed from miles around the area.

Luckily there was no loss of life, although brigade equipment received considerable damage. Mr Peerless' employees lost their tools in the blaze, and they put the value of these at £300.

Reported in the local papers a few months later that the townsfolk had raised some monies. This was with the help of concerts and public donations. They could give the workmen who lost their tools, money to replace them. There was money remaining for the fire brigade with fifteen pounds to replace burnt hoses etc and ten pounds towards the new Engine Fund.

At a meeting of the Local Board held in the Vestry-room in early March 1876. Captain Towner advised they should move the fire escape. He suggested they should place it by the north-east side of St. Saviour's Tower. And advised that it needed repairs. The Board agreed to his requests.

In December, the *Hastings and St. Leonards Observer* reported that Eastbourne had bought a new steam fire engine from the London company, Merryweather & Co. They housed the new engine named 'Fire King' in the Central Engine House in Langney Road. At this time there were two brigades working in the town. The Local Board operated one in Grove Road and the other, a private brigade, in Langley Road, which had bought this new Steamer engine.

Eastbourne Volunteer Fire Brigade.

BALANCE SHEET TO DECEMBER, 1874.

Cr.	£	s.	d.
His Grace Duke Devonshire	2	0	0
Lord Edward Cavendish	1	0	0
R. Insoll, Esq., £1, J. Swift, Esq., £1 1s.	2	1	0
Hon. Mrs. Gilbert,	1	1	0
Miss Brodie,	1	1	0
Albion Hotel Company	1	1	0
Mrs Curling	1	1	0
County Fire Office, per Mr C. Diplock	1	0	0
Norwich Fire Office per Mr J. Brown	1	0	0
The Rev. H. R. Whelpton, St. Saviour's	0	10	0
The Rev. J. Wood, Trinity College	0	10	0
Mrs Oliver, Trinity Place	0	10	0
Mrs Cumberledge	0	10	0
Mrs King, 5s., Mr Whiteland, 1s.	0	6	0
Mr J. Newman, Anchor Hotel	0	5	0
Mr Page 1s., Messrs. Head and Tanner 5s.	0	6	0
Mrs Chapman	0	1	0
Mr H. Sutton, 5s., Mr A. Cooper, 2s.	0	7	0
Russell and Co., 5s., Mr Coombes, 2s. 6d.	0	7	6
Messrs. Cunningham, 5s., Mr Kensett 2s 6d	0	7	6
Mr Bindon, 5s., Mr S. Hall, 5s.	0	10	0
T. Devonshire, Esq. 5s, Mr G. Thatcher, 5s	0	10	0
Balance of Prize from Crystal Palace	0	13	9
1874, part collected to balance 1873 account } His Grace Duke Devonshire, £2, Lord Edward Cavendish, £1, R. Insoll, Esq., £1, F. C. S. Roper, Esq., £2 2s.	6	2	0
	23	0	9

Dr.	£	s.	d.
Balance due to Secretary	0	6	3
Amount drawn as per bills by Capt. Brown	6	19	6
Supt. Mihill	0	14	6
Fireman Jasper for boots	0	3	9
Mr Stevens, harness maker	0	1	9
Mr Piper, shoemaker, Old Town	0	17	5
Mr J. Huggett, for oil	0	1	5
Mr Bartholomew, for caps, &c.	3	12	0
Mr Greenfield, for boots repaired	0	4	0
Mr C. Bradford, for horses	1	5	0
Messrs Merryweather and Sons	6	19	6
Mr J. Fuller, for stationary, stamps, and books	0	4	11
Messrs. Adams and Stevens commission for collecting	1	2	9
Cash in hand of Secretary	0	8	0
	23	0	9

Auditors { J. G. PEERLESS, D. PERRY, THOS. FULLER.

JAMES TOWNER, Captain.

WILLIAM NEWMAN, Secretary.

E/B Gazette 15 April 1875

This private brigade came about because several people in the town were dissatisfied with the firefighting equipment in Eastbourne. They formed a committee with Thomas Fuller and bought a larger Manual engine from Merryweather & Co. This was just before the disastrous fire at the Peerless yard. After this, they decided they required a more powerful Steamer engine and arranged an exchange with Merryweather & Co of their Manual appliance for a Steamer. This private brigade comprised twelve men, a hose cart and other small appliances. Mr J. Hounsom, who joined in November 1897, was part of this brigade. Collections and subscriptions from the public supported them.

Merryweather Steamer　　　*ESRO*

The *Eastbourne Gazette* published the brigade's balance sheet for the year ending 1876. They did not list the assets, but there was a list of all contributions received from gentlemen and women in the town and insurance companies.

Receipts from concerts totalled £57. 15s 3d. Disbursements showed horse hire from Mr C. Bradford, with miscellaneous expenses for tailor, shoemaker, coal, and stationery. There was also an amount paid to Mr Daws for rent on the engine house and expenses paid to Hailsham.

With the new 'Fire King' Steam engine, they decided that practice should take place at Devonshire Road and Seaside Road on Easter Monday 1877. The Steam section of the Fire Brigade then moved to Victoria Place and after lighting the fire, it took nine minutes for the engine to reach 70 to 100lbs per inch pressure and be ready. Their hose projected water some 150 feet from Grand Parade into the sea, which amused the passing residents.

Again, in May, a demonstration took place near the Skating Rink. In June they took the Steam engine to Old Town for a half-hour practice and display for the local inhabitants.

There would be the second annual Volunteers Fire Brigade competition. Which they were going to hold at Alexandra Palace in London on 2nd July

The Eastbourne crews were hoping to attend and expected about sixty fire engines and crews from sixteen brigades to compete in various competitions. The Board agreed to the brigade to represent the town, and they travelled to London. The Eastbourne Brigade won 2nd prize, and six pounds, in the wet drill competition.

In March 1878 and after an increase of men into the Manual Section, Mr Towner, the Captain launched an appeal in the local newspaper for extra funds. The money they were receiving from the authorities did not cover the brigade's costs. He asked the public to contribute. They would use any monies collected for supplying equipment to the men. The Steam section of the brigade was also having a few monetary problems. They had returned a report for the two years ending Christmas 1878 with a deficiency of £148 8s. They too were looking for some voluntary help from the public.

EASTBOURNE (MANUAL) VOLUNTEER FIRE BRIGADE.

The Committee, feeling the absolute necessity of increasing the number of Firemen for the efficient working of the above Brigade, have recently enrolled several new members. The funds in the hands of the Treasurer being quite inadequate for the purpose of providing the equipment needed for the additional staff, the Committee venture to appeal to the public for support. Contributions may be handed to Mr. ALF, the authorised Collector, or forwarded to me, by whom they will be gratefully acknowledged.

(Signed)   JAS. TOWNER,
        Captain of the (Manual) Brigade.
March 25th, 1878.   ——
Sum required for new Boots and Tunics, about £25.

Eastbourne Gazette 3 April 1878

In the same report, they advised they had installed a system of electric bells. Together with telephone connections so they could notify the crews immediately of a fire.

After receiving their new hose reel, the Steam Section of the brigade met at Langney Road fire station for a practice drill. They proceeded to Mr Towner's premises in Terminus Road and fixed a stand-pipe and attached three deliveries.

Two were two-and-a-half-inch canvas hoses and the other a half-inch hose, and they reported that water delivery was good. After a while, they left and went to a screw plug outside the Railway Hotel. Here they attached the large hose with two deliveries. For half an hour, they practised and threw water over the hotel roof. They then turned the water off and returned to the Langney Road station house. The new hose reel was light and manoeuvrable and could easily be manhandled by two firemen. They were pleased with their new asset.

Mr Edward Hollingham owned the Golden Hop Brewery in Langney Road when a fire was discovered on the premises. This was on Friday evening on the 7th of June at about 1 a.m. Two coastguards and a patrolling police officer noticed smoke coming from the boiler room of the brewery. And they immediately dispatched a messenger to the nearby fire station in Langney Road. There was a problem raising any help. But eventually, the watchman despatched the hose reel to the fire whilst waiting for more firefighters to attend. By the time the men had brought the hosepipe to the scene, the building was ablaze. The firemen had to contend with the added danger of exploding beer barrels. The Army barracks engine was first on the scene and assisted. But they and the town engine couldn't save the building, which was consumed by the fire.

The Steam engine arrived and had to unhitch the horses so they could return with the Manual engine. By the time the Steam engine got fired up, the whole brewery was alight.

One of the brewery workers managed to get into the basement and shut off the gas main. He luckily escaped injury when the floor and roof caved in around him. It was ten minutes to two when the brewery roof collapsed. Soldiers and police formed a line around the firemen to keep onlookers away. They estimated that the brewery had sustained more than £3,000 of damage in the blaze. Although the fire destroyed the brewery, they praised the firefighters for their efforts in saving adjoining buildings.

Hailsham Fire Brigade joined the Eastbourne Manual Section on Monday evening, 12 August. This was for practice of their equipment and training for their joint crews. They started at six o'clock for a two-hour session which took place on the Grand Parade. Afterwards, they returned to Grove Road station and then on to the Gildredge Hotel for supper. Also, that evening the Steam Section of the Brigade put on a display for H.R.H the Grand Duke of Hesse. He was entertaining Prince Arthur, the Duke of Connaught. Captain Fuller and his men in full uniform and brass helmets laid outstretches of the hose and played the water onto Highcliffe House, Grand Parade. This attracted large crowds who enjoyed the show.

Monday, September 2nd, and the Eastbourne Brigades received an invitation to the Swiss Gardens in Shoreham. This was to attend a grand fete and competition. They held this for the benefit of the Brighton Town Fire Brigade Building fund.

Brigades and over 300 firefighters from around Sussex attended. Eastbourne came away with third prize in the fire engine practice.

A very interesting letter appeared in the *Eastbourne Gazette* on 25 September. Mr Fuller, Captain of the Steam Section of the Brigade, was the author. He was bringing to the town's notice that the brigade's fire escape ladder had not been brought into use at fire alarms or in any drills since 1873.

There was a tragic fire in Birmingham, recently reported in the newspapers, and the fire crew at the scene found their escape ladder to be defective, lives were lost. To avoid such a tragedy happening in Eastbourne, he suggested that the Local Board should rectify the situation. Mr Fuller had brought this matter to the attention of the Lighting Committee before, but they thought it was unnecessary to take any action. He suggested that the Parish Brigade had failed in their duties. He proposed that they should delegate two firemen from each section as Escape Conductors. He also thought they should instruct the police in the use of the fire escape ladder. This arrangement was current in other towns such as Hastings, Brighton and Croydon. Also, they should inspect the ladder and if necessary, get it repaired.

By writing this letter, it appeared to have stirred up a hornet's nest. The Captain of the Manual Section, Mr Towner, demanded an apology and threatened to take action for libel.

Mr Fuller has since inspected the appliance and found it in satisfactory order. Even though the escape is old and of an obsolete pattern, he found the arrangements of its use and management needed attention. The local paper supported Mr Fuller and his comments on the fire service. But they suggested that it was time the Board amalgamated the two brigades and placed them under one commanding officer. They accused the Local Board of bias towards the Manual Section and that they should reconsider their position.

Before they built the Meads Street fire station, the brigade stored their fire escape ladders in churchyards in the Meads area. This was a practice used in many towns in England. They used Trinity Church in Seaside first, then from 1878 until 1894 they used the St. Saviour's churchyard. From 1895 until 1907, they used facilities at St. John's Church.

Saturday 28 December, the Manual Section of the brigade went to the Crumbles to practice for a single-man and double-man drill competition that would take place on New Year's Day. A few days later, in early January 1879, the Manual Section of the brigade with Captain Towner attended a grand supper at the Gildredge Hotel in Terminus Road. They had recently held a fire drill competition on the cricket ground at Clifton House School, South Fields, and the supper was a celebration of the event. Prizes were given out, and in the speeches, they mentioned that there had been some "unpleasantness" between the Steam and Manual Sections. They hoped both parties would come together in a "friendly way".

February 5th and the *Eastbourne Gazette* related a report presented to the Eastbourne Volunteer Fire Brigade. In it, the Steam Section issued their accounts. This was for the two years ending Christmas 1878. To make the section free of debt, they required £148 8s. and called upon inhabitants to support them and help clear the debt.

Eastbourne's Volunteer Brigade attended the Lord Mayor's Show in London in early November 1880. The Fire Brigade Association had invited them and fifteen other brigades to take part in the procession through the capital's streets. After the parade, the Lord Mayor and Sheriffs gave a dinner. They held this at the Anderton's Hotel with Colonel Sir Charles H Frith, the president of the Fire Brigade Association hosting the evening.

The Local Board held a meeting at the beginning of May 1881. Mr Towner (a member of the Board and Captain of the Fire Brigade) reported that the service attended four calls to fires in the last year. The Lighting Committee had held three inspections, and they had supplied a new larger hose and hose reel. It was also noted that they had supplied a new electric bell system. He did not mention whether this was the one that Mr Fuller had installed for the Steam Section. Nor had they installed the system of fire bells at both fire stations. Mr Towner had also mentioned that a "more convenient and drier engine house was needed". This remark referred to the Grove Road fire station. The Board noted his comments and promised to pass them onto the Lighting Committee.

Drills and practice are normal for the firefighters. And on Monday 17 October there was a drill competition which they held in a field near Hartfield Square, Upperton Gardens. The Eastbourne Manual Section commanded by Captain Towner attended, together with guests from the Hailsham Fire Brigade. Local business owners acted as referees and timekeepers.

Since the setting up of the Hailsham fire service in 1877, there had been a friendly working relationship between the Eastbourne and Hailsham Brigades.

Different events took place during the day with drills for one man, two men and four men teams. There was also a fifty-yard race with a ladder and a bucket of water. One prize given was a silver helmet that Merryweather & Co of London had donated for the one-man drill competition. H. Newman Jnr, of the Eastbourne Brigade, won this prize together with winning the fifty-yard race.

At the Local Board meeting in November, the brigade handed a report to the Committee stating that the Engine House needed repairs. They estimated it would cost about fifty pounds for the works. They also received notification that there was still a problem with wet and dampness in the building. The consensus was they needed a new fire station.

At the beginning of the month, on the 9th, they held the funeral of Inspector William Bryant. The London, Brighton & South Coast Railway Co (Brighton Line), employee was a well-respected man in the town working at Eastbourne Railway Station and as a volunteer fireman.

They carried his coffin on Eastbourne Fire Brigade's Manual engine, with both Captains' Towner and Fuller in full dress uniform attending. Many other dignitaries were present, including representatives from Hailsham Fire Brigade and colleagues from the railway union.

Two horses died, and considerable damage caused to stables when a fire broke out in Roselands near the Recreation Ground, in Pevensey Road. This was on Friday 24 November 1882. A passing police officer discovered the fire at four o'clock in the morning and raised the alarm. They rescued two carts even though they had sustained serious damage. Before they discovered the fire, the horses had died. Captain Fuller and his crew rushed to the scene with hose reels. And shortly after, Captain Towner and the Manual engine arrived. The wind was gusting, and the engine couldn't be of any help. There was no hope of saving the building. Besides the hay, straw and harnesses destroyed, workman lost their tools in the fire. The tools stored in the barn were being used for installing paving in front of the Recreation Ground.

Mr J. Compton Merryweather and Mr John Robbins, a fire engineer, were staying at the Queen's Hotel and requested Mr Fuller to wet drill his Brigade. Merryweather's had supplied a Steam fire engine to Eastbourne in 1876, and they wished to see how it performed.

So, on Monday afternoon, 26 March 1883, outside the Queen's Hotel, Captain Fuller and his team connected hoses to hydrants. They sprayed water at the hotel at a rate of 300 gallons a minute, with jets of water reaching 125 ft even in the strong winds blowing at the time. Mr Merryweather's party were very pleased with the performance of the engine, and after an inspection, complimented Capt. Fuller for his team's performance and the way they had maintained the fire engine.

Reported in the local papers in May: the fire brigade had now established electrical communications. This was between the Grove Road fire station and the Steam Section in Langney Road. And they also made connections to the local messengers and turncocks.

Late on Sunday evening, the 17 June, a passer-by discovered a fire at the bakehouse belonging to Mr J. Hammick, in Carlisle Road. Captain Fuller from the Langney Road station received the call at 9.10 p.m. and was on the scene within fifteen minutes. On arrival, he found two hoses manned by men from Devonshire Park. They contained the fire to the interior of the building and extinguished it in less than an hour. However, there was water in the basement up to 4ft 6in deep, which hampered the clean-up.

The principal damage was to the flour stock, although the walls and floor suffered from smoke and water damage. Captain Towner did not receive a call to the fire until 9.40 and when he arrived, the fire was under control.

****

1912 Eastbourne's first motor fire engine.   *ESRO*

Early 1900s cap badge.

Pre 1974 cap badge. EFB ring in red.

When the town was hosting prominent or royal visitors, it became customary for the brigade to put on a special display. They would form a large archway with their fire escapes. Then they would decorate this with bunting, buckets and firemen would stand in full uniform on the escape ladders. This would be a welcome to the visitors and demonstrate their ability and professionalism to the town residents.

Sometimes the Bicycle Club and Fisherman's Club would also construct large arches for the visitors.

1883 June Visit Prince of Wales. Grove Road.

Heritage Eastbourne

1929 Prince of Wales Visit. Terminus Road

3 COUNTY BOROUGH OF EASTBOURNE

Eastbourne received its Charter of Incorporation of the Borough on 16 June 1883. On the 1st November, they held the first Eastbourne Council election. The following year, 1884, the Council established the new Borough of Eastbourne Fire Brigade. The council rates would now support the service.

After Eastbourne became a Borough, there were many changes to the fire service. The Borough arranged the hiring of horses for the Steam Section for one year with Mr A. Bradford. Mr J. Tobutt would supply the Manual Section. The question came up about fire coverage of the outlying parishes around Eastbourne. They agreed that these parishes would have to pay an annual charge for the Eastbourne brigade to attend. The fee was three guineas each for the parishes of Pevensey, Westham and Willingdon. Alfriston parish applied but had their application refused. The Council considered the village too far away from the town. Although the parishes paid a subscription there were strict rules applied on when the Eastbourne Fire Brigade crews would attend. The brigade's fire captain had the authority to decide if his men would travel to a fire. If he considered it necessary, he could ask the landowner of the land that the fire occurred on to pay for the attendance of the brigade. Should they receive a call to a fire in Eastbourne, then that would be their priority.

In the early hours of Friday 25 January 1884, a fire broke out at the shop of Messrs. Hope & Co. They were wholesale window blind manufacturers in Junction Road. The shop was next door to a warehouse containing oils, paint and paper hangings. With tenants living above the premises. Two young men living on the first floor were awakened by smoke in their bedroom, and discovered the fire and contacted the fire service. They then alerted other residents and their children and helped them to evacuate the building. One of the young men ran off to the nearby fire station in Langney Road and rang the fire alarm. Some firemen departed at once to the fire with hoses.

The water supply was good, and they promptly attached a hose to the hydrant. The brigade's Steam engine arrived on the scene in less than twenty minutes. They informed Captain Towner at the Grove Road station of the fire, and he set off with the Manual appliance.

When the men from Grove Road arrived, they attached a second hose to the hydrants. The firefighters were able to tackle the fire from both the front and rear of the building as there was a lane running at the rear of the shops.

Firemen had brought the escape ladder along but did not need it, as tenants had vacated all persons from the building before the brigade arrived. With the help of the Steam engine, the fire did not spread to adjoining shops. The ground floor shop of Messrs Hope & Co. was burnt out, and the bedrooms immediately above sustained serious damage. The fire had originated in the back shop and destroyed a cart and the entire stock on the premises. They estimated the total financial loss at a little under £700.

Because there was no telephonic way to contact the firemen living in Old Town, they would usually send a messenger. But this morning he was ill, so they did not help in the firefighting. Just as well, as there was also a fire that morning in a furniture warehouse in Ocklynge Road, Old Town. Luckily, they discovered and extinguished the fire without a need to call out the brigade.

On Wednesday 20 February, the Council Borough Surveyor and other officials tested the efficiency of the two fire brigade stations. They gave no warning to the brigades of their inspection. Some Council officials took up positions opposite the shop to observe proceedings and the effectiveness of the men. At seven o'clock in the evening, they advised the stations that a fire had broken out in a shop in Cornfield Place. They sounded the alarm, and within eight minutes the hose reel from Grove Road arrived. At 7.16 at full gallop, the Steam engine from Langney Road arrived and ten minutes later was pumping water. The Manual pump from Grove Road did not arrive until 7.30, and it was ten minutes before it was in use. After some minutes they told the crews to pack up their equipment and return to their stations. The officials sent a detailed account of the evenings' drill to the Committee. A few days later, Eastbourne's local newspaper carried a report of the exercise.

After the February drill, the new Borough invited the Inspector of Brigades to visit and test the brigade's efficiency. He was Capt. G. R. Wykeham Archer, the Vice-President of the Fire Brigades' Association.

On 19 March, at 11.45 p.m. a call went out saying there was a fire in one of the hotels in town. The men turned out, and they brought out the escape ladder from St. Saviour's churchyard. Afterwards, Captain Wykeham Archer forwarded a report to the Town Council. He noted that the Manual engine from Grove Road arrived within four minutes after they received the alarm and the Steam engine from Langney Road eighteen minutes later. He considered that the brigade's turn out "to be most satisfactory in all particulars".

In April, after a meeting of the Committee in which Captains Thomas Fuller of the Steam Section and Captain James Towner of the Manual Section attended. They decided they had to change the way they organised the brigade. The Corporation stated they should have more control over the brigades and would take over the service from the Local Board. The amount outstanding on the purchase of the fire engine in Mr Fuller's brigade was thirty-four pounds. And the Council agreed to pay for this.

They would then find suitable premises for housing the appliance. Mr Fuller had informed them he had the authority to hand the engine over to the council. He advised them that the engine and equipment had cost eight hundred pounds. The Corporation also agreed to pay nine pounds a year and a house rent-free for two resident firemen and the expenses for the horse hire, coal, gas, together with wages of four pounds a year for the remaining firemen. Uniforms for both Manual and Steam Sections would be the Council's responsibility. They would maintain all expenses out of the public rates, and the brigades should stop collecting subscriptions from members of the public. The Corporation agreed to set up a Committee of Management. For a short while, the brigades had two Captains. James Towner of the Manual section and Captain Fuller of the Steam section.

In May, Alderman Pearson asked the Council for permission for the Fire Brigade Committee to pay suppliers. The amount was £23 10s. And this was for urgent repairs needed on the Steam engine. The Council agreed to his request.

At the meeting of the Buildings Committee on the 15 July, they were still discussing Mr Fuller's amended plans for a fire station in Cavendish Place. They adjourned the matter. However, at the October meeting, they agreed to rent the property offered by Mr Fuller in Cavendish Place as the new fire station.

The Fire Brigade Sub-Committee at their meeting in October confirmed the arrangement. They recommended the Council should take a lease for fourteen years at fifty pounds per year. That was not the end of the matter as further amendments were made and agreed at the February meeting in 1885.

Reported in the *Eastbourne Gazette* of 6 January 1886 at the Fire Brigade Committee meeting last December, they reached an agreement about the hire of horses. They accepted the tender from Messrs F & A Bradford to hire horses to the Steam Section and the tender submitted from Mr J. Tobutt for the hire to the Manual Section. This arrangement was for twelve months from the 1st January 1866. They agreed in the future they should leave the question of horse hire to the discretion of the fire captains.

A young girl died in her bed in a fire in the early hours of 24 November 1886 when a house and shop in Seaside Road were gutted by a terrible blaze.

Charles J. Venus, a fireman at Devonshire Park was passing the premises on his way back from work when he noticed smoke coming from the rear of the building. They sent a messenger to the fire station in Cavendish Place whilst Venus, with the help of neighbours evacuated some members of the family. Witnesses claimed they tried to save the girl who was in an upstairs bedroom, but the smoke and flames drove them back. The hose reel from the Steam Section was first to arrive, followed shortly after by the reel from Grove Road. Captain J. Towner received information about the fire at ten minutes past two and dispatched his hose reel team. At the same time, they sent men to St. Saviour's Church to bring the escape ladder, which took twenty minutes to arrive. They used two fire engines and the escape at this tragic fire.

Fireman Arthur Turton, who received the call about the fire at 2.20 a.m. arrived at the scene and found the hose reel working and directed onto the fire. He climbed the ladder and fought his way through the smoke three times before he could rescue Mr Longman's daughter, Eleanor. At the inquest, he said that he thought the girl had already died from smoke inhalation when he found her. Many people complained that had the Council sited the fire escape in the east end of town they might have saved the young girl's life. They said Eastbourne only had two fire engines and one escape ladder and with its many shops, tall buildings and hotels the town should have more adequate cover.

This was not the brigade's finest hour. It had taken almost half an hour to manhandle the heavy escape ladder to the fire, and they positioned the young girl, head downwards when they placed her into the escape chute. A hook ladder holding the chute broke, and the casualty hit her head on the ground. The later report of the fire in the Eastbourne paper shocked people. London papers published an account of these events. The following day the Board sanctioned the purchase of some small escape ladders. They also approved the building of a hose drying tower at Grove Road station. The estimated cost of this was seventy pounds.

Around this time there had been a lot of fires in Eastbourne. On 2 January 1887, a significant fire broke out at two o'clock on Sunday morning. It was in a large upholsterer's shop belonging to Mr Edward Pearce. A passing police officer heard the sound of breaking glass and fire and without delay raised the alarm. Within eight minutes, crews from both Cavendish Place and Grove Road were on the scene with their hose reels. A few minutes later the engines arrived, but their services were not required as the firefighters could control the fire with their hoses. They safely evacuated the residents of the property (nine in all). But soon the flames were shooting through the roof, and neighbouring buildings were in danger of being caught up in the fire.

Because of the quick action of the firemen, only the shop and a neighbour's stores suffered damage, although that was extensive. The estimated cost of the damage to the shop and stores was £2,000. The tenant of the shop and landlord were both insured.

Later in the month the Board received and tested two escape ladders built by Messrs E. H. Bayley & Co. These had cost the Council £100. They positioned them near the fire stations in Grove Road and Cavendish Place. The new escapes are of the same design as ones used in the larger towns throughout the country.

The fire crew at Cavendish Place used to hold regular practice sessions on Monday evenings, starting at 6 p.m. They would bring out the Steam engine into the road and light the boiler to get steam pressure up to pump water. They fed regular-sized logs of wood into the fire-box, and with a shudder, the engine would come to life. Smoke would then billow out of the shiny brass chimney. Sometimes the crews would manhandle the escape ladder to the Congregational Church in Pevensey Road, which they used as a practice tower.

They would extend the ladder up the church tower and men would climb the ladder. On occasions, they would fix a hose to a hydrant and they would run this up to the top.

With essentially two fire brigades operating in the town, and both responding to fire alarms, but without conflict, the question of which one was senior at the scene of a fire arose. They brought the matter up at the March meeting of the Fire Brigade Committee. Captain Towner attended the meeting when they agreed that each captain should have control over his relative section. When both sections attended a fire, then Captain Towner as the senior officer should have overall command. There was no complaint about the brigades, but they hoped that this would clarify matters.

On Monday 4 April, the Mayor (Lieut. Col. W. A. Cardwell) at the Town Hall presented Fireman Turton with a silver medal and a cheque of three guineas. The trustees of the Society for the Protection of Life from Fire awarded this gift. This was in recognition of his bravery last November at the tragic Seaside Road fire. Mr Turton thanked the gathering for their support and said that he was just doing his job. He would share the cheque with his comrades who were with him that day.

Also in April, the Fire Brigade Committee approved plans for Merryweather & Sons to repair and overhaul the Steam fire engine. Merryweather had quoted £92 15s. for the work. Whilst their Steam engine was being repaired, they hired a Steam engine from the company, at an agreed price of £5 per week. The repairs were expected to take between one month and six weeks. At the meeting, they agreed to take out insurance from the National Boiler Assurance Company for the Steam engine. This would be at an annual premium of £1 13s.

There was a large fire in Devonshire Place on Friday 20th May. A house, known locally as 'Merlin', a stone constructed building belonging to Miss Bell, received extensive damage. The blaze destroyed the roof. As the house was well known, and the fire broke out on a Friday afternoon, hundreds of people from all parts of the town flocked over to watch the spectacle. They raised the alarm to the fire brigades at about two o'clock and Captain Towner with the Manual engine arrived promptly. Seen by the crowds, there was a lot of confusion and lack of decisive orders. This together with problems with the brigade's hose pipes, which were leaking, caused a delay in tackling the fire. Shortly after the men arrived, the entire roof was ablaze with debris falling all around with the fire working its way downward. The Cavendish Place Steam engine had recently returned from London after repairs and did not arrive at the house until an hour and a half after the Manual engine.

It was early evening before everything was under control, some four and a half hours after they had discovered the fire. Both Captain Towner and police Superintendent Newnham had lucky escapes. Whilst they were standing on the upper staircase, it collapsed, they did not sustain any injury. But the attic and second floor suffered considerable damage in the blaze.

The firemen believe the cause of the fire to have been the overheating of one of the chimney flues from the kitchen. An estimate of the destruction caused was over £2,500.

Fortunately, the occupants had the house insured for £4,000 and the furniture for £1,000. The local newspapers repeated the residents' demand that the Council should abolish the dual control of the fire brigades. It suggested that the Council should re-organise the fire service and it should come under one authority with just with one fire officer in overall charge.

Merryweather brought their new fire engine, the Oxford Jubilee, to Eastbourne for a trial with the firm's Mr J. Compton and Captain Cleaver travelling down for the demonstration.

At their meeting in January 1888, Mr Hounsom suggested and arranged the setup of an Accidental Fund. This was to help any of the volunteer firefighters should they have an accident at work. A few years later, at the annual meeting in January 1890, they renamed the fund as the Sick Benefit Fund.

Hastings and St. Leonards Volunteer Fire Brigade have an annual outing for its crews and in June 1888 they decided to visit France. As part of the group to travel to Boulogne, they invited members of the Eastbourne Volunteer Fire Brigade to send along a few of its men. Captain James Towner led the Eastbourne group with John Towner, John Easter, Mr Fowler and Mr Brown.

On arrival in France, they were all entertained with fire drills by the local crews who turned out in full uniform. Dinner and some local entertainment then followed. The firemen themselves funded the entire trip with no monies taken from brigade funds.

At the Fire Brigade Sub-Committee meeting of 19 December, they agreed to accept an offer from Messrs W. and J. R. Newman for a new fire station in Watts Lane, Old Town. They would build the premise and the Council would take out a lease for seven years at twelve pounds per year. The council also agreed to erect a lamp outside of the building.

Eastbourne Council produced its annual accounts for 1888/9, and the expenditure for the Fire Brigade was £363 5s 2d. Wages for the Steam and Manual Brigade came to £114 with £56 7s for the Telephone Company. The balance was for tradesmen and equipment for the men.

It was not all work and drills for the fire crews. On Friday 19 July 1889, there was a visit to Eastbourne by H.R.H Princess Helena, the Duchess of Albany, Queen Victoria's daughter-in-law. She was visiting the All Saints' Convalescent Hospital in the Meads. Mayor Alderman Bolton and other dignitaries accompanied her. There was bunting in the streets, and the roads were crowded with spectators. They all cheered as the royal visitor drove through the town from the station. Opposite the Gildredge Hotel in Terminus Road, the fire brigade created an arch. This was with two fire escapes and near the summit, they formed a balcony with scaling ladders. They decorated the whole arch with small flags, leather buckets, and hoses draped over the rungs of the ladders.

The crews were in full uniform manning this. On either side of Terminus Road, they placed their Steamer and Manual engines, which produced fountains of water that pleased the crowds. When the Duchess and her party left in the afternoon, the firemen acted as guards of honour at the railway station.

Captain Towner led the brigade out for the annual 'Mayor's Night' and bonfire celebrations on Monday 11 November. They proceeded through the town with their Steamer drawn by four bays. The Manual engine pulled by a pair of horses followed this. His men all turned out in full dress uniform and the Bonfire Boys followed them. The whole procession with bands and musicians marched throughout the town and the carnival did not finish until after midnight.

This was a busy month for Captain Towner. He received a diploma and gold badge from the French Fire Brigade Service, and they made him an honorary member.

The Fire Brigade Committee met in January 1890 to consider three tenders received for a new Steam fire engine. The tenders received ranged from £300 to £500, and the Committee agreed to refer the matter to the Borough Surveyor and Captain Towner. In April, Merryweather & Co submitted their tender for a new fire engine. At the next council meeting. The Mayor moved a motion to adopt the decision of the Fire Brigade's Committee. And accept the tender received.

A serious fire occurred on the morning of 21 May at Mr S. Smith's drapers' shop in Seaside Road, and there was extensive damage to the premises and stock. Whilst fighting the blaze, Fireman Terry sustained an injury as he was adjusting the position of his hose. It struck the firefighter's hand, which caught some broken glass in a door. It was a nasty cut and needed attention from the doctor. He could not attend work for some time, and the Sick Benefit Fund awarded him 15sh per week. Although they did not use the Steamer engine at the fire, they used their hoses. The estimate of damage to the building and stock was £1,500 and £2,000.

After much debate in Council, they ordered a new Steam fire engine from Merryweather & Sons in London. It was a Horizontal Greenwich model, which they delivered in mid-August.

Wednesday 1st October saw a public display of the new engine. They drove it to the Town Hall where the brigade put on a display of the power and reach of the engine and hoses. They sprayed water on the building, which reached the roof. Then they connected another hose and simultaneously threw water on the building. The Mayor, after a brief speech and smashing a bottle of champagne, tied to the engine by a coloured ribbon. Named the engine, 'Morrison'. Alderman Sutton then performed a similar ceremony on the old engine. This they named 'Sutton'. The 'Morrison' was then formally handed over to Captain Towner. Afterwards, they served light refreshments to council members in the Mayor's parlour.

In March 1891, severe storms and blizzards hit the town. The storms interrupted communications and for a week telephone connection between the police, fire station and firefighter's homes were affected. They stationed men in the fire station overnight in case of a call out. But soon workman had repaired the wires. There were no major fire incidents reported during this period.

On Saturday 21 June, the Prince and Princess of Wales visited Eastbourne to open the new Princess Alice Hospital. On their arrival at Eastbourne station, sizeable crowds greeted them.

The fire brigade erected an arch on Terminus Road made up of two fire escapes and scaling ladders decorated with flags. Underneath the arch, they positioned the Steamer fire engines with the Manual engine in the centre. This then produced fountains of water when the royal couple passed. The firemen had turned out in full uniform, and this was a similar display to the one they produced in 1889.

The German Emperor and Empress whilst on a visit to England attended the large National Fire Brigade event at Crystal Palace held on Saturday 11 July where over 1,400 volunteer firefighters were on parade. Fifty-eight engines from around the country were on display, and most of the Eastbourne Brigade attended.

Captain Towner was honoured when they chose him to be one of the firemen to be presented to the royal couple. The evening concluded with a large firework display.

A few days later the brigade lost a long-serving engine driver, Mr A. Davis, aged 46, who was suffering from influenza and pneumonia. He died at the Princess Alice Memorial Hospital and his coffin was carried on a fire engine to Ocklynge Cemetery. Mr Davis had served seventeen years in the brigade.

There was a devastating blaze on Sunday, 20 December when Ratton Hall, Willingdon owned by Mr Freeman-Thomas J.P. (who was away at the time) caught fire. The house, the second on this site, was a Georgian style property by Sir George Thomas. The fire started at 5.30 a.m. in the upper storeys of the forty roomed Manor House and rapidly spread throughout the entire building.

At once they dispatched messengers to Hailsham and Polegate and a horseman to Eastbourne, asking for urgent help. Both the Eastbourne Steamers and the Manual engine from Old Town attended, but they could not save the building. When the fireman arrived, about 7 a.m. the roof was ablaze and soon collapsed. There was little they could do. Mr Freeman-Thomas had insured the manor with the Sun Fire Office. And they estimated the damage to about £5,000 including the furniture and house. The following day hundreds of spectators turned out to see the damage.

Whilst the firemen were dousing down the embers, they heard a noise. They broke a window and found a badly burnt poodle dog who belonged to Mrs Brooks, Mrs Thomas' daughter. They rescued him and later reported that he survived his ordeal. In February 1892, the brigade received payment of ten guineas for the use of their equipment in the Ratton fire.

Some years later a local company owned by Mark Martin built the third mansion. This was in the Victorian-Tudor style and designed by Frederick G. Cooke. But a fire destroyed this new Ratton Manor House on the night of 23 December 1940, when the Canadian army was in residence.

Ratton Manor

In March, the Committee recorded that Messrs Chapman was now supplying horses for the brigade.

Mr Towner asked permission from the Watch Committee in June to take the Steam engine 'Morrison' to a fire appliance competition. They were holding the event in the grounds of the Manor House, Bexhill, on 7th July. With brigades from Hastings, Lewes, Battle, Normanhurst and Bexhill attending. He also asked for help with his expenses. The Committee approved his requests.

The day out was successful for the Eastbourne brigade, who paraded through the town with the other brigades led by a brass band. They won first prize in the four-man drill and second prize in the two-man Manual engine drill. And shared the first prize with Hastings in the six-man and officer turnout drill. They also secured wins in other classes and it was a profitable and enjoyable day for the crews.

Mr Towner presented his yearly report for 1893, in which he stated there were 23 fires and 3 false alarms reported during the year. The total number of working hours for the brigade was 960, working out at 36 hours per fireman. The estimated loss from the fires was £1,425. They had only used their fire engines at nine fires, as they extinguished the rest with the use of buckets. This was because most of the fires were minor accidents in the home. In only one incidence was the fire escape used when a female was brought out of a burning building. The contractor for the supply of horses was Messrs Chapman and Sons, whose service was satisfactory. The strength of the brigade was twenty-nine, including two messengers. Seven members held St. John's Ambulance certificates. All the fire stations were in direct contact with each other, as well as with the police and the Exchange by telephone. He also reported that there was a balance of £22. 0s 6d in the accounts. The brigade had paid out forty-one days' sick pay during the year.

Late December in the early afternoon there was a fire at a two-storey house in Cavendish Place. Firefighters attended and Escape Foreman Terry tried to enter the building. But he could not gain access because of the smoke and flames.

At last, he gained entry to the premises and pulled out a sixteen stone man from the blazing bedroom. With his fellow fireman, they brought the man down safely. The casualty had received extensive burns and they took him to Princess Alice Hospital. Sadly, the man died a few days later from his injuries. Fireman Terry received acknowledgement for his bravery when the Mayor of Eastbourne presented him with a cheque for one guinea. The Royal Society for the Protection of Life from Fire had given this.

They needed repairs for the 'Sutton' Steam fire engine, and in February 1894 the Board agreed to a quote. This was from Merryweather & Co for £88 17s 6d. In June, after repairs, Merryweather returned the engine.

Sunday 30 December 1894, the *Eastbourne Gazette* reported the death of 39-year-old Fireman Arthur Turton. On Boxing Day, he attended the meet of the Eastbourne Foxhounds and was in good health. It is thought that he caught a chill, as on Saturday he went to bed, and the family called the doctor. But he passed away at half-past ten on Sunday morning. The doctors said nervous influenza caused his death, followed by paralysis. Besides being a volunteer fireman serving for fourteen years, he managed the Meads Grocery Stores. Mr Turton leaves a widow and seven young children, the eldest only thirteen years of age. They carried his coffin on a fire engine with many of his fellow firemen in attendance and held the memorial service at St. John's Church in Meads. Interment was in Ocklynge Cemetery. The Captain of the brigade, James Towner, started a fund to assist the family. He also sent a letter to the Committee requesting help. A short while later, he reported that they had collected over £150 for Mr Turton's relatives.

May 1895, the Watch Committee suggested that they should establish a fire station in Meads.

On 20 November, the Duke of Connaught visited Eastbourne. He was attending a meeting and banquet with the Provincial Grand Lodge of Sussex Freemasons. The town greeted him with the streets festooned with flowers and bunting and the fire brigade erected an arch. They constructed the arch in Compton Street with two fire escape ladders and a platform. Fifteen firemen in full uniform stood on the rungs of the ladder. The Steamers, 'Morrison' and 'Sutton' were at the base. The fishermen also erected an arch at the Grand Parade.

In the early hours of Sunday morning the 12 January 1896, Mr Stephen Daw, discovered one of the largest fires that Eastbourne had seen for many years, whilst walking past some workshops. The building yard of James Peerless in Langney Road was ablaze. Twenty years earlier in 1874, there had been a huge fire at the yard which many of the current firemen had attended. The yard and two-storied building were burning, and there was substantial damage. Two horses died, and the fire destroyed a spring van and dogcart. The estimated loss caused that day was £4,000. Eastbourne's fire engines 'Morrison' and 'Sutton' had attended the fire, together with men from Meads and the Old Town fire station. The firemen were at the scene until after midday Sunday.

During this year, Mr Towner retired from the service because of ill health. He had completed twenty-five years with the Eastbourne Brigade after joining in 1868.

In recognition of this, the council made him Honorary Captain of the Brigade. In March, the Watch Committee considered George Gausden (a builder of Langney Road) to succeed him.

In mid-April, the Mayor convened a meeting as there was disquiet in the fire service. This was about the Captaincy of the Brigade. Finally, after much debate and subject to the approval of the Watch Committee, they decided that the Mayor would become Captain. The Senior Superintendent would be Mr G. Gausden. With Mr J. A. Hounsom as Superintendent.

The Committee hoped that all concerned would accept their decision. At the May meeting, they confirmed the agreement with arrangements made in April.

Robert Sumsion

In the annual May carnival of the Battle of Flowers, held on Tuesday the 19th, Superintendent John Hounsom and the Steam engine 'Morrison', drawn by four horses, won a cheque for five guineas. This was for the best-decorated fire engine. They had decorated the engine with arum lilies, laburnum, bluebells, stocks, narcissi and moss with a palm set in the funnel. A day of relaxation for all the crews.

On account of heavy usage, the Sick Benefit Fund was running out of resources, which became challenging. At the annual meeting of the brigade, a member suggested that they should hold a Firemen's Ball to help their financial situation. The membership agreed to this idea. This annual event has turned out to be very successful and helped raise funds for firemen in need. The Ball has been held annually now for many years.

There were mutterings in the local newspaper about the efficiency of the fire brigade. They pointed out that every year a government official inspected the Police Force. They suggested there should be an inspection of the local fire brigade carried out by "someone holding a high position in the Metropolitan Fire Brigade". This was just the thoughts of the journalist. But action was taken some years later.

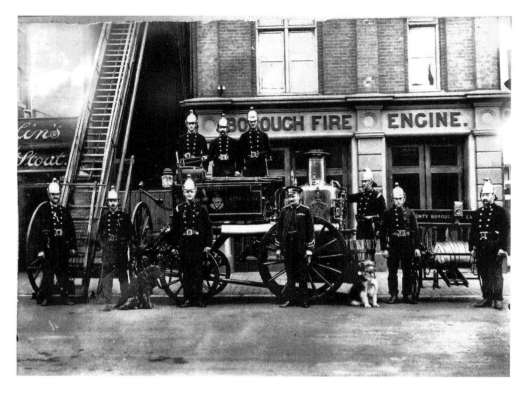

Outside Cavendish Place Fire Station. *Robert Francis*

In September the Council approached the Local Government Board for finances to buy the land of the Cavendish Place Fire Station. They were now leasing the land and building from Mr Thomas Fuller at fifty pounds per year. And he was offering it to the Council at nine hundred pounds freehold.

The current lease would expire on 25 December 1900, and the new rent would increase to sixty or seventy pounds.

The council had considered buying some land offered in Seaside. But the firemen had advised that they wished to stay at Cavendish Place. Nine members of the Cavendish Fire Station had sent a letter to the council urging them to either renew or buy the lease. They stated that the current arrangement was useful as most of the firemen lived close by the fire station. And Mr Chapman, who supplied the horses, had his stables nearby. The building, constructed by Mr Fuller as a fire station, was brick built with a slated roof and was in excellent order. A few months later, the Town Clerk confirmed at the March Committee meeting that they had completed the conveyance of Cavendish Place.

In November, at the Watch Committee meeting, ratepayers representing Mead's area presented a memorial demanding "a Fire Escape or other means of protection for Meads". There had been an escape ladder situated by St. John's Church, but that had disappeared. The nearest ladder was at St. Saviour's Church.

The residents of Meads were still waiting for the council to build a fire station in Meads. The Mayor replied they had ordered a new escape ladder and when they receive it, they would send one of the three escape ladders to Meads. Plans for the new fire station were still being discussed. And they hoped that they would conclude soon.

There have always been storms in Eastbourne, but the south-westerly gale of the night of Tuesday 2 March 1897, was one of the most severe to hit the town. This storm caused devastation and destruction right across the county. From South Wales and Dorset to Gravesend and Lowestoft, towns experienced severe damage.

The storm wrecked boats, damaged piers, blew telephone wires down and disrupted postal services. In Eastbourne, it washed away part of the timbering on the new seawall. Some of the wooden structures hit the 'Birdcage' bandstand, and two of the iron columns supporting it were broken and dislodged from the bandstand. There was severe damage to the Grand and Queens Hotels and the Parish Engine House. Like Bognor railway station, the storm blew the roof off the Parish Engine House building.

It blew part of the lead roofing of the fire station into the air, which landed in the street by Grove Road and Ivy Terrace. They estimated that the piece on the ground weighed about a quarter of a ton. Spectators soon gathered around and cut pieces of the sheet of lead as souvenirs.

Some years later, Chief Fire Officer Phillips acquired one of these inscribed pieces of lead. This was a piece a quarter of an inch thick about 2 ½ ins by 1 ½ ins. Someone had engraved it with the words "Piece of roof of Hose Reel House, old fire station, Grove Road blown off in 1897". Mr Phillips added it to his collection of fire brigade memorabilia. This storm follows on from an earlier storm in December 1896, which caused major damage to the seafront. That one deposited over two hundred tons of shingle onto the promenade. The fire brigade spent all day pumping out flooded premises in the town.

The Building Surveyor had completed plans for the new fire station in Meads and submitted them to the Watch Committee on 26 March. Then they requested him to obtain a quote for a new hand hose reel carrier for the Meads station. At the 23 April meeting, the surveyor advised the Watch Committee that he had received an estimate from Messrs E. H. Bayley & Co Ltd. This was for £12 15s 0d and they agreed it was acceptable. They requested that he should arrange the purchase for a pair of copper lamps for the cart. Also, to have the words 'Borough of Eastbourne Fire Brigade' written on its side. The revised total bill for the cart was £15 10s 0d inclusive of the lamps that had been requested. At the October meeting, they agreed to forward payment to Messrs Bayley.

Wishing to keep up with advances in the fire service, the Fire Brigade Sub-Committee at the April meeting agreed that Mr Hounsom and Councillor Foran should travel to Tunbridge Wells fire station. They would then report to the Committee about any recommendations they conceived.

In Willingdon, they held a meeting in the parish hall on 13 April. They suggested that to mark the Diamond Jubilee of Queen Victoria, that they should invest in the village's own fire engine and hoses. They thought this would be of significant advantage to the village. And the village would not be just relying on the Eastbourne Fire Brigade.

The meeting agreed to this and arranged door-to-door collections from the residents to raise the necessary funds. After the purchase of a second-hand Merryweather hand-operated engine. They formed the Willingdon Fire Brigade with sixteen men under the command of Captain Charles Carter.

On the 22 June, there were grand celebrations for the Diamond Jubilee. And the new fire engine named 'The Willingdon' was on parade.

Villagers and children followed by a drum and fife band marched into a field, and Captain Carter and his Brigade gave a display for all the villagers. The village presented Captain Carter with a whistle, and two of his men with winches.

There was a large fire brigade jamboree in July, which they reported in the *Eastbourne Gazette*. There were 1,500 firefighters from around the country with their fire engines and ladders attending. They held the meeting at Home Park, Windsor. To inspect the brigades, they had invited Her Majesty the Queen. Presented to Her Majesty was Superintendent Hounsom. Together with Engineer Perry, Escape Foreman Reed, Reel Foreman Payne and Fireman Hobbs. Sixty to seventy fire appliances were on show, and there was a torchlight procession in the evening.

Finally, in August, the Watch Committee agreed to buy land offered by the Compton Place Estates for the new Meads fire station. The agreed amount was £195. They then instructed the Building Surveyor to advertise in the local press. He invited tenders for the construction of the new fire station. And the Building Surveyor received five tenders from builders for the Meads station. The one from Mr J. C. Lacey at £575 was the lowest and accepted subject to the necessary contract and bond being entered into to. The Committee then arranged in October to borrow the monies from the Local Government Board. They also mentioned at the meeting, that the cost of hiring horses from Mr Bradford was 45/- for each false alarm and £1 1s per fire.

In late 1897 the Fire Sub-Committee appointed John Hounsom as Captain of the Eastbourne Brigade. Mr Hounsom as sub-engineer and subsequently Superintendent had joined his brother in the Volunteer Fire Service in 1878.

At the end of January 1898, the South Coast District of the National Fire Brigade Union held their annual meeting at the Town Hall in Bexhill. They elected Captain J. Hounsom as Vice-Chairman for the coming year.

Thirty-two members of the fire brigade assembled in front of the Townhall on Monday 23 October. They were to be inspected by Mr Webb. He was a former Superintendent of the Metropolitan Fire Brigade, and the Watch Committee had invited him to Eastbourne. This was on a recommendation from Commander Wells, R.N., Chief of the London Brigade.

On display were the fire engines, 'Morrison' and 'Sutton', the Manual engine, four reels, a hose cart and three escapes.

Mr Webb filed his report, stating that the discipline and general bearing of the fire crews were satisfactory, and complimented Mr Hounsom for his well-drilled men and state of equipment.

He recommended that the latest pattern telescopic escapes should replace two of the escape ladders. He also suggested that they should instal four more fire alarm points for the outlying districts.

The Fire Brigade Sub-Committee met, and afterwards, the Watch Committee approved plans for Captain Hounsom to get quotes from Messrs Merryweather, Shand Mason and More & Co for two light 45ft telescopic escapes. The maximum cost approved for the two escapes was £130. They also required an estimate of the cost for a covering for the fire escape at the Cavendish Place fire station. Regarding the fire alarm call boxes, they would deal with this matter at a special meeting of the sub-committee.

At the Watch Committee, Captain Hounsom presented his first annual report, which they reported in the local newspaper in March 1899. This covered the year ending December 1898 and stated that the brigade had received thirteen calls for attendance within the borough, and two from outside the area. There had been seven false alarms recorded and compared to last year, that was an increase of four fires. He estimated that the total loss from fires this year was about five hundred pounds. With the total number of working hours for the brigade at 960. He also reported that because of high tides they used the Steamer 'Sutton' to pump water out of the 'Windsor Tavern'. The total strength of the brigade stood at thirty-two, and they have installed electric fire bells at fireman's homes. One member of the crew is on duty at Grove Road and Cavendish Place stations each night from seven until ten o'clock.

He was pleased to advise that seven members hold certificates from St. John's Ambulance and fifteen members having 'Long Service and Good Contact' medals from the National Fire Brigades' Union. The report continued with details of 130 day's sickness paid out during the year costing £9 15s 0d. Messrs Chapman and Sons supplied the horses, and they attended to them very well. Captain Hounsom estimated the value of engines and equipment was £1,561 17s 6d. This did not include the premises but included two Steamers, one Manual engine, fire escape ladders (3) and hose carts with hoses. Members attached to each fire station stood at Grove Road 11, Cavendish Place 11, Old Town 5 and 4 at the new Meads fire station. Captain Hounsom recommended they should class the fire station in Grove Road as their primary station. He thought they should sell Cavendish Place station and suggested that they should provide a new fire station in Whitley Road.

The local papers reported the death of Thomas Fuller. He had been Captain of the Steam section of the Eastbourne Fire Brigade and had served for seventeen years.

In 1888 he moved to Petersfield in Hampshire and passed away on the 2nd of March. His body was transferred to Lewes Station on the 7th and met by fireman in full uniform. The coffin was placed on No. 2 engine from the Cliffe section.

His funeral took place in Cliffe, with many members of the Eastbourne and Lewes Brigades attending. They buried Mr Fuller in the All Saints' and Cliffe cemetery.

There was a large competition held in Devonshire Park on 17 May, which the South District of the Fire Brigades' Union organised. Present at the show were brigades from the Brighton Volunteer and Railway, together with Hastings, Hove, and Burgess Hill. Also, the brigades from Lewes, Newhaven Town and Harbour, Hailsham, Haywards Heath and Worthing fire stations. There were many drills and exercises during the day, and the Eastbourne Town Orchestral Band entertained the spectators. Eastbourne crews won the new 'Eastbourne Challenge Shield', which was in the Steamer drill competition. This entitled them to represent the South District of the Fire Brigades' Union at the forthcoming National Union Competition in Birmingham.

Later in May, the Fire Brigade Committee met to discuss raising funds for the firemen who wished to attend a large exhibition in Paris. It agreed that the men could advertise for subscriptions from the public to help with their expenses for travelling to France. The Committee also discussed they required another Steam engine to protect the town as the current engine was old. Earlier, fifteen or eighteen months ago, they had carried out repairs to the old engine for one hundred pounds. They established they would need about five hundred pounds for the purchase and agreed to find a second engine.

July and Eastbourne hosted the Sussex Agricultural Show. The Prince of Wales was to open the show, and he arrived by train on Saturday evening. After the usual greetings at the railway station, the official party set off for Compton Place. By the Town Hall in Grove Road, the fire brigade set up the two new telescopic fire escapes. They formed an arch decorated with canvas hoses, buckets and various other utensils and manned by thirty firemen. Both the 'Morrison' and the 'Sutton' Steam engines were on display and they positioned the Manual engine at the base of the arch.

August 12th and the Eastbourne Brigade received a call to a sizeable fire in Willingdon. Park Farm in Willingdon belonged to Mr William Carter where they had just finished harvesting on Saturday. Later that evening they discovered the fire. Mr Carter was a respected member of the Eastbourne Board of Guardians and a member of the Rural District Council. Although the Eastbourne and Willingdon fire crews were working until late, they could not save the barn. Lost in the blaze were machinery, oats and wheat, but the cattle survived. Hundreds of residents in Seaside, Upperton and Ocklynge came out to watch this huge blaze that lit up the night sky. On Sunday, sizeable crowds visited the farm.

In the *Eastbourne Gazette* on the 16 August, a fireman calling himself "The Old Cinder" from the Cavendish Place fire station was venting his anger.

This was about unpleasant remarks made about the fire service. He stated that when the station received the call at 10.55 p.m. about the fire, they had wanted to leave immediately. But as the fire was in Willingdon and outside of their area, they had to wait for authority to attend. All the firemen could not attend, as this would have left Eastbourne without cover.

There were many people outside of the fire station abusing the firemen for not departing at once for Willingdon. When at last they received their authority, the firemen finally departed at 11.55 p.m.

There are many instances when the service receives a call out and cannot help. One such occurred on the evening of Wednesday 27 September. Eastbourne fire service received two telegrams for help from the Hailsham Brigade. They found horses, and with eight firemen they rushed to the scene, arriving within the hour. A fire had started in a carpenter's shop, spread to the bakers and then onto the Post Office. The fire did not demolish the Post Office, but there was extensive damage caused by water. The postal staff abandoned the building and found new premises for the mail services. When the Eastbourne engine arrived, they found that there was only one hydrant close to the fire. Superintendent Whitlock of the Hailsham Brigade informed them that their help was no longer required. So, they returned to Eastbourne at 3 a.m. after a wasted journey.

Eastbourne Fire Brigade had a rule book for its firefighters and a copy turned up at the Bicester Urban Council meeting in November. They suggested they should adopt certain hints in the book and print them in their book of rules.

****

Heritage Eastbourne

Grove Road and the fire station with hose drying tower

1896.   Senior Superintendent George Gausden

1896.   Superintendent John Hounsom

4 NEW CENTURY

In January 1900, Captain Hounsom presented his second annual report to the Watch Committee. This was for the year ending 31 December 1899. He stated that the brigade had received sixteen call outs to fires within the Borough and one outside of the area. There were also six false alarms, five chimney fires and one brigade test making twenty-nine calls for the year. The total loss and claimed from insurance companies was £1,785 4s, more than the previous year. Their engines only got to work on one fire as they dealt with the others with water directly from hydrants. All equipment was in good order, and a crew member was on duty from seven until ten o'clock at each of the four stations. The brigade has a strength of 40 men, with 33 connected with electric fire bells fixed at their homes. Seven members held St. John Ambulance certificates, and 17 have 'Long Service and Good Conduct' medals.

He said that the new fire station at Meads was "a great addition to the district". During the year they added two new 50ft Telescopic fire escapes to the equipment. With one at Cavendish Place and the other at the Meads station. He confirmed that on advice from the Committee, he had divided the Borough into four districts for fire calls. This year they had paid out 256 days in sickness benefit. The Sick Benefit Fund for the Brigade stood at £81 6s 4d, an increase on last year. Messrs Chapman and Sons still had the contract for horse hire. And finally, he estimated the value of all engines, escape ladders etc to be £1,689 17s 6d.

The Willingdon Brigade was working under extreme difficulties. They sometimes had problems finding the horses to draw their fire engine as they also used them on the farms. It was not unheard of for the crews to pull their fire appliance by hand and arrive at a scene of fire exhausted. Even then the pressure of water through their hoses was very low and they could only extinguish the smallest of blazes.

Their engine was not the most efficient machine, and after attending a few fires they raised doubts about its efficiency. In February, they decided to sell the Merryweather. They had stored the engine in a barn for many years, and it became derelict. It finally was sold as scrap to a metal dealer.

Once again, the village came under the cover of the Eastbourne Fire Brigade. The only large blaze that the recently established Willingdon fire service had attended was the fire at Park Farm in August 1899.

They reported in the newspaper that Captain Hounsom had sent a letter for publication. In it, he suggested Willingdon should keep its fire engine. He stated that as one did not know when there would be a serious fire that they should consider the retention of the appliance. Or alternatively they should buy a more powerful one.

After a successful Fireman's Ball in May, they announced that they had paid all the expenses, and there was a surplus of £16 15s. This amount would go to the Fireman's Sick Benefit Fund as this needed support as there were now over forty members. The following month the brigade with their Steamers, 'Sutton' and 'Morrison' took part in a large procession along the seafront. A pair of horses pulled each engine, and the Manual appliance accompanied them. Sixteen members of the brigade all in blue uniform and brass helmets rode on the engines. This parade was in celebration of the christening, by the Mayor of the new lifeboat, '*William Stevens*'.

Also, in May the firemen collected some money for colleagues who were away fighting in the war. They arranged for Captain Hounsom to buy some sweaters for Mr T. Crowhurst and Mr T. Gosden and the brigade forwarded them to their comrades.

In August, Paris hosted the International Congress of Firemen and invited twelve hundred representatives from brigades around the world. Besides the members from England, there were delegates from many other countries. Including the United States, Belgium, and Sweden. Also, Portugal and Norway. Captain Hounsom represented the South Coast District of the National Fire Brigades' Association and travelled to France with his colleagues Superintendent Perry, Sub-Engineer Reed and two other members of the brigade.

On their arrival in France, there was a reception held in Boulogne which the Mayor hosted. The following day they were guests of the Mayor of Versailles who treated them to a "sumptuous" banquet. During the week there were drills and exhibitions of the latest firefighting appliances and equipment. When the congress ended, they were all treated to dinner at the Palais Royal before departing Paris on their journey home. To their delight, their hosts after the meal presented gold-enamelled medals to the officers.

September saw a fire in Westham when at 7.30 p.m. smoke was seen coming from the stables and coach-house of the Railway Hotel. They called the brigade, and the 'Morrison' engine arrived at about 8.50. The firemen soon extinguished the fire, but the flames destroyed the building and the hay and straw in the stables.

They reported this incident in the *Eastbourne Gazette*, a few days later. A fireman from Cavendish Place fire station sent in a letter of complaint to the newspaper. He stated that they were ready to leave for the blaze half-an-hour before the Grove Road crews, but they were ordered to stop and could not attend.

Chimney fires were a constant worry for the fire brigade. Because householders did not check and have their chimneys regularly swept, there were always many call outs to extinguish these fires. To encourage householders to be more responsible, they drew up laws and the local magistrate would summon and fine anyone who had a chimney fire. Local councillors had fallen foul of the law, and in March 1901, they summoned Mr Hounsom, the captain of the Eastbourne Brigade, to court. A police constable about 4.50 p.m. on March 12 noticed that the dining room chimney was on fire and called the brigade. Mr Hounsom advised the court that they cleaned his chimney last November, but the Bench fined him 2s 6d.

Captain Hounsom presented to the Committee in March 1901 his annual Fire Brigade report for the previous year. They had received twenty-one call-outs to fires within the Borough and just one outside the area. Most of these resulted in minor damage, but four fires suffered losses of £400, £350, £200 and £110 worth of damage. He supplied no further significant details to the Committee.

Engineer Harry C. Newman had recently retired from the fire service after serving for over thirty-five years in the brigade. In recognition of his long service, his fellow team-mates wanted to give him a gift. So, on Saturday 19 October, they arranged a presentation at the Cavendish Place fire station. Captain Hounsom presented him with a silver cigar case on behalf of all his colleagues.

Mr Newman applied to the Watch Committee for a grant as he could not work because of an illness that he maintained he sustained in the service. They held a meeting in December and suggested they would pay a grant of six pounds. This amount was equal to one year's pay in the fire service. After discussions with the fire Captain, the Committee agreed to make a grant of ten pounds to Mr Newman.

Captain Hounsom produced his fourth annual report in March 1902 to the Watch Committee. Advising that the brigade received twenty-one call outs to fires in the year 1901. These included two false alarms and two chimney fires. The largest damage recorded in an incident was £1,700, with the rest under £400. They had spent a total of 1,470 hours attending fires, and that equalled forty-nine hours per man. They only used the Steamers at two fires as water from hydrants, and the hand pumps were enough at the rest. He was pleased to report that the strength of the service was forty men. With one other still away on active service.

Seventeen of his men held 'Long Service and Good Conduct' medals and seven had St John Ambulance certificates. The Committee agreed to approve an order to fix a fire bell at Fireman Newman's house in Old Town.

Also, at the Watch Committee meeting, they agreed to accept the tenders they had recently received. These were for new uniforms for the Fire Brigade. Messrs Atkinson & Co, London, were to supply the Captain's and Superintendent's tunics. Together with trousers, jackets and fatigue caps. They would also supply Firemen's belts. Messrs Menhinick White Ltd would supply the Engineer's, Sub-Engineer's, Foremen's and Firemen's tunics as well as trousers and caps.

At the April meeting of the Committee, they discussed the concern that Grove Road fire station needed repairs to the roof. Walls required attention and the front wall and doors needed painting. They referred the matter to the Sub-Committee.

The Brigade was happy to host a visit from the Chiswick Volunteer Firemen on 13 June. There were twenty-five firemen and three town councillors at the party. At lunch at the New Inn Hotel, they discussed the advantages of a tall hose drying tower at their station. The Eastbourne men were impressed with the organisation of the London station. Chiswick was one of the best-equipped fire stations in London with a resident engineer. Their horses were always ready for service.

Eastbourne's suburbs were expanding and, on 12 August, the Borough invited former Liberal Prime Minister Lord Rosebery to visit the town. This was for the formal opening of Hampden Park and the newly constructed King's Drive. Lord Rosebery was the president of the 'Liberal League' and a close friend of the Duke of Devonshire who could not attend the ceremonies. There was a grand ceremony, followed by lunch at the Town Hall. After lunch, everyone travelled to King's Drive for the opening ceremony and the cutting of a blue and yellow ribbon. The fire brigade had erected an arch across the road with two escape ladders and adored with fire apparatus. Firemen stood in full dress uniform on the ladders. Afterwards, everyone travelled to the entrance of Hampden Park for the official opening of the new public park.

The Fire Brigade Sub-Committee in September agreed to make enquires for temporary accommodation of the fire engine or the cost of a temporary erection of a fire station.

Plans were progressing for the New Technical Institute and Library. And on the 8 October, there was a sale of the buildings that they were going to demolish. Mr James Vine was successful for the purchase and agreed to pay £26 for the three buildings. Within a few days, they had demolished the Vestry Hall, Fire station and a cottage.

Although there was opposition to a new fire station in Grove Road. They agreed on plans in November with the architect Mr Philip A. Robson of Bridge Street, London. (He was also responsible for drawing up plans for the Technical Institute and public library in Grove Road).

The Watch Committee originally recommended to the Council acceptance of a quotation from Messrs W. & E. Neakes for the erection of the new fire station. This was in June, and again, in July 1903. But they did not award the company the contract as they could not supply the guarantees that the council requested.

Robert Sumsion

In November, and the Committee reported that the rent paid to W & J. R. Newman was £7 0 8d, and they paid the Gas Company £3 16 7d. These were expenses for the fire station in Watts Lane, Old Town. While W. M. Caffyn & Sons received £15 to cover the half-years contract to attend to the fire alarms at all stations.

In March 1903, Captain Hounsom at the Committee meeting suggested that, as they were considering providing public baths for Old Town, they should consider the building of a new fire station in the same scheme. The Committee rejected his plan.

At the beginning of April, the brigade took delivery of a new Merryweather 'Curricle' Escape ladder. One man could handle this lightweight machine. The ladder could travel horizontally and had a reach of 40 feet.

On the 25 April, there was a grand ceremony when the Duke and Duchess of Devonshire came to Eastbourne. The visit was to lay the foundation stone at the New Technical Institute. The Mayor and most of the council greeted them at Eastbourne railway station. At the ceremony in Grove Road, were Eastbourne's Freemasons and local businessmen. This was a grand affair with processions in the street. The Duke had given the land to the town for the New Institute, and the town rewarded him by making him the first Honorary Freeman of the Borough. Captain Hounsom was by the fire station with his men, all in splendid blue uniforms, complete with axes and shining brass helmets.

They had erected an arch made up of four fire escapes, with the two Steam fire engines at their base. Then they draped hoses around the arch.

THE DEVONSHIRE PARK.

NATIONAL FIRE BRIGADES' UNION.

THE ANNUAL

DISTRICT COMPETITIONS

Will be held as above,

THIS DAY (WEDNESDAY), MAY 20th,

Commencing at Two o'clock sharp.

The splendid "Eastbourne" Challenge Shield and Worthing Challenge Cup, will be competed for, also competitions to qualify for the National Events at Earl's Court in July, in Steamers, Manuals, Fire Escapes, Hose Carts, &c. Also a Popular Programme of Sports.

A Band will be in Attendance.

Admission £d. Subscribers Free. Enclosure 6d. Extra.

May saw another competition held in Devonshire Park. This was for the Eastbourne Challenge Shield and Worthing Challenge Cup. The winners would qualify for the prestigious National Events at Earls Court in July.

E/B Gazette 20 May 1903

Perhaps it was a quiet news day, but the *Eastbourne Gazette* of 23 June ran a worrying story about the brigade. "The Fire Brigade will change its name to Water Brigade. It will leave the extinguishing of future fires to the rain, and will reserve its energies for pumping out tradesmen's cellars". Were the recent floods on the south coast the reason for the brigades change in direction?

The Duke and Duchess of Devonshire hosted a private visit for King Edward VII on the 11 July 1903. The King had visited Eastbourne before as Prince of Wales and agreed to receive reception from the town and its dignities. After arriving at the railway station, the royal party drove along Cornfield Road where the Eastbourne Bicycle Club had erected an elegant triumphal arch. Twenty-five members of the Club positioned themselves and their bicycles at the base of the arch. Further along the route, in Devonshire Place, the Fire Brigade also erected a lofty arch. They used three escape ladders, and the Steam engines, 'Sutton' and 'Morrison' were at the base. The Royal Party then proceeded to Compton Place.

January 1904 and the Borough Surveyor informed the Watch Committee that the old parish fire engine was still being used and was not installed at the fire station as previously instructed. They informed him they would deal with the matter.

Captain Hounsom presented an interesting report in February. This was his sixth report and covered the period up to December 1903. It was a quiet year for the brigade with sixteen calls to fires. Fourteen were in the Borough and three outside the Borough. Although the total monetary loss was slightly greater than the earlier year, the heaviest financial loss in one fire was £240 against £335 in the previous year.

Statistics for the last six years showed 1898 at £499 10s, with the property at risk £7,438. To the highest in 1901 at £3,035 11s, with the property at risk £19,740.

The Captain advised the Committee that he had taken responsibility for the care and training of staff at the Grand Hotel and arranged supervision of the fire appliances on the pier. Also, he recommended the brigade should carry out regular fire drills in all the schools and hotels in town.

Whilst on the way to a shop fire in Hampden Park in September, the Steamer was involved in an accident. It collided with one of the gates at Hampden Park and one of the pair of horses sustained an injured. There was damage to one of the poles of the Steam fire engine. When they finally reached the fire, the shop had completely burnt out. But they saved the neighbouring buildings from damage. The estimated cost of the of the fire was between £500 and £600.

At the October meeting of the Town Council, they approved final plans and alterations for the new fire station. Part of the alternative plans provided for an office and showroom, 11ft 6ins wide and 60ft deep with a room above and a basement. The Council had arranged for The Electric Light Company to rent this at sixty pounds a year. This would be their central office with space for exhibitions and savings on their present accommodations.

The brigade held its ninth annual ball on Monday 13 February 1905 at the Town Hall. This was to raise funds for the Sick Benefit Fund. The Mayor and other officials attended with music from the Municipal Orchestra. Tickets for the ball were 3s each, and the dancing and drinking carried on until 3.30 a.m. the following morning.

Mr Philip Robson produced plans for the new fire station which the Council approved in June, although there had been some objections to the plans. The new building would be on the site of the old Vestry Hall, the small cottage and the old fire station. Since the demolition of the old Vestry Hall building and Parish Engine House in October 1902, the fire brigade moved in June to the old Market House in Grove Road. They allocated half of this building for the brigade and set aside the other half as a temporary home for the Free Library and Reading room.

They drew up a lease between Mr William Hudson and the Corporation with a rent agreed at £100 per annum. This was not an ideal situation, but the current landlord was only using the building for storage. This gave the Grove Road fire crews a short-term home. The council then arranged for advertisements in the local newspaper for tenders to build the new fire station. Sixteen companies replied, and they awarded the work to the local builders, Peerless, Dennis & Co.

On a drizzly Sunday the 24 September, the Fire Brigades National Union held a procession and a march through Eastbourne. They were advertising and collecting contributions from the public. This was for the National Fire Brigades' Association Widows' and Orphans' Fund. The crews and visitors, about eighty firefighters, assembled with two brass bands at the Grove Road Fire Station. One band was from the 1st Sussex Royal Engineers. And the Postmen formed the other. Representatives from brigades around the South Coast District attended. The day began with a service at St. Saviour's Church. During the day, they collected under twenty pounds for the fund.

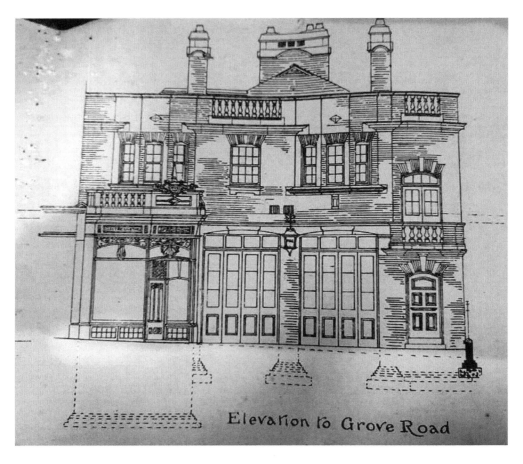

Elevation to Grove Road

January 1905 Drawing. *Gavin Barsley*

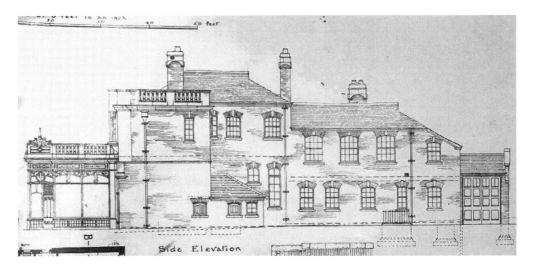

Side Elevation

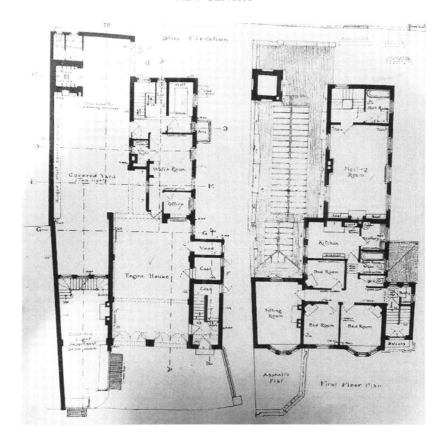

January 1905 Drawings. *Gavin Barsley*

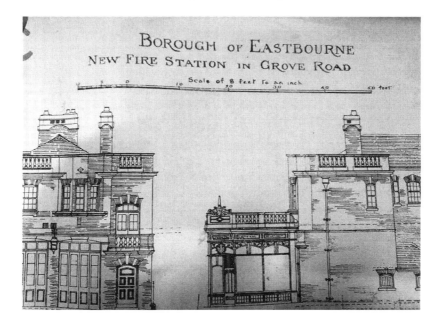

WATCH COMMITTEE.

Thursday, 12th October, 1905.

PRESENT—

Mr. Alderman DUKE (Chairman).

Aldermen ROWE and TOWNER.

Councillors BRADFORD, CLIMPSON, FEAR, HOLLINS and RAWLES.

1. MINUTES.—The minutes of the last meeting of the Committee having been printed were submitted, and the Chairman was authorised to sign the same as being correct.

2. NEW FIRE STATION.—Tenders for the erection hereof were submitted as follows :—

Mr. Mark Hookham	5,423
Mr. Wm. Burgess	5,354
Messrs. Norman & Burt	5,195
Messrs. James Wood & Son	5,190
Messrs. Martin, Wells & Co.	5,150
Messrs. John Garrett & Son	5,084
Messrs. Strange & Sons	5,077
Messrs. E. Cornwell & Son	5,062
Mr. Joseph Martin	5,050
Messrs. R. Cook & Sons	4,914
Mr. F. G. Minter	4,912
Messrs. Miller & Selmes	4,847
Mr. A. J. White	4,834
Messrs. J. Longley & Co.	4,768
Messrs. Peerless-Dennis & Co.	4,747
Messrs. Rowland Bros.	4,659

Resolved : That the Council be recommended to accept Messrs. Peerless-Dennis & Co.'s Tender at £4,747, and to affix the Common Seal to the necessary Contract, and that the necessary Capital Expenditure be referred to the Finance Committee.

An application by Mr. Wm. Noakes for appointment as Clerk of Works was read and deferred.

Top row: G Prodger, fireman Towner, fireman Murrant, fireman Ridley, Escape foreman Fosden, Sub engineer Crowhurst,

Second row: fireman Moss, fireman Eldridge, fireman Dinnage, fireman W Newman, fireman Ticehurst, fireman F Newman, fireman Harmer, fireman Hodson, fireman Button, reel foreman Tunbridge.

Third row: fireman Pagden, fireman Gosden, fireman Lewis, fireman Knight, fireman Myhill, escape foreman Collins, fireman Coombe, fireman Hunt, fireman N Prodger, fireman Terry

Fourth row: F Dopson, A Newman, G Terry (Hon Sec), S Weakford, J Newman, J Hounsom, T Browning, F Newman, S Garnham, H Newman, H Diplock and Fireman Miller.

Colin Fox

The brigade had many drills and inspections, and on Monday 30 October, ex Superintendent Stutter of the London Fire Brigade visited Eastbourne. Thirty-six of the men turned out. Three men were missing the inspection because of ill-health.

They had arranged for the inspection to be outside the Town Hall. But because of very inclement weather, they held it at the Arcade in Grove Road. The Mayor and chairman of the Watch Committee also attended. They placed four escape ladders against the Town Hall with hoses run to the hydrants and brought in the Steam engines. The firemen then carried out various drills. When they had completed the drill, they went into the Town Hall for refreshments. After tea, Captain Hounsom again spoke of the necessity for a new fire station in the town.

A few days later, the Watch Committee received Mr Stutter's observations. His report stated approval of the excellent way that the fire stations, police, and chief officer were connected to the fire call boxes by the electric bell system. He noticed it connected every fireman up to his respective fire station. All the local telephone subscribers had to do was call number 13 to gain help. There had been suggestions they should convert the Manual engine to carry a 65ft telescopic ladder. He considered it unnecessary and advised that a motor fire escape and first-aid appliance would be preferable. This they could buy at a reasonable cost.

In his report, he said that the eastern and north-eastern part of town was expanding and would soon need more cover. He noted that in the previous year there were fifteen fires recorded. He was satisfied to see all Steamers, escapes, reels, hoses and other appliances were in good repair and correctly maintained. In conclusion, he said, "in every way, your brigade can be considered thoroughly efficient, and compares more than favourably with other brigades".

After much discussion at Council, building started on the new fire station in Grove Road. This was behind the New Technical Institute. They agreed to rent out part of the building to the Borough's Electric Lighting Department for their offices and a showroom.

Local builders began work in January 1906. They built the new building in red brick, and it stood two-storeys high with a slatted roof. There was a square-shaped, 45ft hose drying tower at the rear. The building could house two fire appliances together with ladders and hoses. Automatic doors supplied by Shand Mason helped for a quick exit. There were sizeable rooms for the crews to relax in together with bedrooms and bathrooms. Also supplied was a large glass covered yard for drills and engine maintenance, with a small basement at the rear. There were not any stables at the new fire station as times were changing and motor engines were becoming the norm although it was some years before Eastbourne had their own motor fire engine.

The eighth annual report from Captain Hounsom stated there were only sixteen reported fires in the year ending December 1905. The total loss recorded was £701 14s 2d. He also reported that in 1905 they lost some 370 days because of illness and the fireman's Sick Benefit Fund had paid out about £29 in compensation.

On 26 May 1906, they chose Captain Hounsom to travel as one of the local representatives of the National Fire Brigades' Union. He was to visit Milan, Italy. Lieutenant-Colonel Fox from the London Salvage Corps led the group. After leaving Victoria Station, they arrived in Boulogne, where they received a champagne welcome from the local brigade. Onward to Paris, where several members of the Paris Brigade joined them for dinner at the Gare du Nord railway station restaurant. After, they caught a train to Milan, where they finally arrived on Sunday morning at six a.m.

This was a large congress, and they presented all delegates with a silver medal. The Italian Federation also gave everyone a silver badge with a red and white ribbon. There was a fire appliances exhibition and representatives from sixteen countries took part in a display. On Thursday 31 May, they held a competition. Whilst in Italy their hosts treated them to excursions to some local sites of interest, which included a trip to one of the nearby lakes.

On the 4 June, Captain Hounsom, with Mr Strickland from Hailsham and some other firemen extended their stay. They travelled to Rome, Florence and Venice before returning to Milan and their journey home. The *Eastbourne Gazette* on 13th and 27th June reported the firemen's journey.

On a wet Saturday 3 November, the Mayor and Mrs Fox at four o'clock formally opened the new Central fire station. About a hundred persons were present. Amongst the dignitaries who attended were the Captains from Brighton, Uckfield, Bexhill, Hastings with Hailsham, Caterham and Tonbridge Fire Brigades. Together they opened the outer doors of the station with a special presentation key. And the party moved into the drilling hall for a presentation. Speeches were reviewing the circumstances that led up to the erection of the new station.

There was a vote of thanks to the Mayor for performing the opening ceremony. Captain Hounsom responded to the speeches. He said that at this time, the Eastbourne Fire Brigade was supported by forty officers and men stationed in four fire stations in the town. With the new fire station, a fireman would be permanently on the premises to receive urgent calls from the public. Eastbourne had averaged twenty-four fires in the past ten years. Last year the crews spent 140 hours fighting fires. They reported the day's events in both the *Eastbourne Chronicle* and *Gazette*.

A serious fire broke out in the furniture business of Alderman Wenham & Son. The premises were situated at the corner of Pevensey Road and Langney Road. They discovered the fire in the early hours of Saturday 13 April 1907 and raised the alarm at 2.25 a.m. at the Cavendish Place fire station. Captain Hounsom, who lived nearby, rushed to the scene where he found the Steamer 'Sutton', hose reels and the escape already at the fire. The firemen evacuated the residents from the property. Whilst fighting the blaze, firefighters saved fifty to sixty mattresses stored in the building. There were about eighteen firemen in attendance, and as the water pressure and supply were good, they did not use the Steamer. Within half an hour the crews had the fire under control but were at the scene for 2½ hours damping down the embers. Under Captain Hounsom's command, the firemen worked quietly without shouting.

The neighbours living in properties facing the blaze did not know about the fire until they awoke later in the morning. Captain Hounsom estimated the damage to the business to be about £1,200.

In early May, they held the funeral of Reel Foreman Harry Payne. He originally joined the service in 1881 as a messenger and had been a well-respected and long-serving member of the brigade. After the service at All Souls' Church, they placed his coffin on the Grove Road hose-reel (which he had requested a few days before his death) with six of his colleagues attending.

Following were representatives from the Eastbourne, Brighton and Hastings Brigades. There were also officers from Uckfield and Hailsham fire service. They buried him in Ocklynge Cemetery.

After the death of fireman Mr H. Payne, a foreman at the Grove Road station, the brigade issued an appeal in the local newspaper for funds. It was to help his widow and seven children financially.

This was successful, and the *Eastbourne Gazette* of 6 November reported that they had raised a little over £150 with the money coming from collections by the firemen. Together with grants from the National Fire Brigades Union, and the Widows' and Orphans' Fund. Captain Hounsom and Mr Payne's employer also contributed.

In Captain Hounsom's report in October, it said that the heating boiler at Grove Road had sprung a leak. This flooded the engine room, and he had arranged for repairs to the boiler. Also, in his report, whilst at a recent drill, Fireman Towner had sustained an injury. No details were provided, but the brigade submitted a claim to the insurance company.

1908 was a tragic year for the brigade, with three firemen losing their lives during year. No fireman had been lost doing their duties in the last fourteen years. Engineer Frank S. Dinnage had worked at the Grove Road station, and although he was only forty-four, he had been suffering ill health for a while. A plumber by trade, he had served in the fire service for twenty-four years. He was a well-liked fireman and at his funeral in May, officers from Brighton, Hailsham and Uckfield attended. They carried his body to the church on the 'Morrison' fire engine together with his helmet, belt and axe.

Not all calls outs to fires are local. On Saturday the 9 January 1909, the brigade received a call to a fire at Sherrington Manor, which was ten and a half miles away from Eastbourne. They made ready the 'Morrison' engine and decided that four horses were to be used to pull the engine, instead of the usual two, and this delayed their departure. On reaching the scene, they found the Lewes and Hailsham Brigades attending. The Eastbourne crews had received the call to the fire at 5.55 p.m. and arrived at the Manor a little after seven o'clock. When the Lewes fire crews arrived with their Steamer, they found the blaze already extinguished.

There was only damage to a motor car and the garage, but the chauffeur needed medical help, which they administered. The Eastbourne engine returned to Grove Road fire station, arriving back in Eastbourne about 10 p.m.

Hailsham, in this period, rarely had sizeable fires. But in early January 1910, they received notification that the mill situated one mile outside of the town on London Road was on fire.

The large mill and outbuildings owned by Horsebridge Roller Milling Co. Ltd were located on a three-acre site by a stream. At 11.50 a.m., the workmen on site discovered a raging blaze and attempted to put it out, but could not control the fire. They sent a messenger to Hailsham fire station and telephoned the Eastbourne fire service for help. The Hailsham Manual pump arrived twelve minutes after being advised and found the mill in a mass of flames. Eastbourne received the call about the mill at 12.20 and arrived on the scene one hour and five minutes later.

At about 2 p.m. part of the roof collapsed, and it was not until 3.30 p.m. that the fire was under control. There were no casualties but substantial damage to the buildings. They estimated that the cost of the fire to be £5,000. This was not the first time the mill had suffered a major fire, as twenty-five years earlier they had a similar incident.

Torquay Town Council did a comparison of yearly costs of maintaining a fire service. They carried a report of this in the *Eastbourne Gazette* 24 August 1910. Nine towns were in the report which covered towns such as Bournemouth, Brighton, Coventry and Acton. Eastbourne was the second-cheapest at £683 with a population of 50,000. The highest was Brighton at £2,833 with a population of 130,000. Coventry, Bournemouth and Ealing costs were all over £1,000 per year. The most modest per 10,000 population was Oxford with Coventry and Bournemouth with a lower cost per population than Eastbourne.

At the 1910 December Sub-Committee meeting, Captain Hounsom, in his report, requested that they should consider the safety and fire cover requirements of the Hampden Park district. He stressed the need for additional cover in that area. The pressure of the water was good, but there was a need for more hydrants. He suggested that at least four fire alarms should be set up with direct communication with the Grove Road station. Also, they should recruit four local men into the fire service. With the 1910 Eastbourne Borough Council Act, Hampden Park and parts of Willingdon now came under the auspices of the Borough. Although it was some years before they built a fire station in Hampden Park.

Captain Hounsom also advised the Committee that they should move the 'Morrison' Steamer engine to the Meads fire station. This would aid with the continuing demands for help towards the Downs and call outs to gorse fires.

He brought the matter of the purchase of a motor fire engine up in the meeting and suggested the type and model that the brigade required. He estimated that the cost of all these improvements would be about £1,200.

It had been some years since there was a serious fire in Eastbourne, but all changed on Tuesday 17 January 1911. When at 9.20 p.m. the police received information about a fire at a drapery shop in Seaside Road. They at once contacted the fire station. The fire brigade at Cavendish Place received the call, and four minutes later they set off with the Steam engine and fire escape. Captain Hounsom was in command. On arrival at the shop, the firefighters observed that the ceiling had collapsed into the shop, and the fire had spread to the upper floors.

By this time there were not any occupants in the building, and the crews went about the business of putting out the fire. In total, thirty-five firemen attended under the direction of Superintendent Browning, together with thirty police constables, whose job was to control the gathering crowd and keep order. The firemen positioned the Steam engine in Susans Road and brought down extra hoses from the fire station. Then they placed the escape ladder against the building with two crew members directing jets of water into the building. The two-storey shop was completely gutted, and at 12.15 p.m. the following day they were still dowsing the flames. Insurance covered the premise and shop contents, and the estimated damaged caused was £5,000.

Following the fire in Seaside Road, the *Eastbourne Gazette* carried an article stating that the fire appliances in the town were out of date and slow. They said that a town the size of Eastbourne should have a motor fire engine that could be dispatched immediately and would not have to wait to get up steam before it was operational. They also noted that Captain Hounsom had brought this matter up at the recent Watch Sub-Committee in December. On the 22 February, they were still writing articles about a motor fire engine, with notes that the London and Glasgow Brigades had already ordered such vehicles. The feeling was that it was about time that Eastbourne had one.

At the Watch Committee meeting in February 1911, Mr Hounsom again recommended that they should buy a motor fire engine. He suggested that the cost would be £950, and this time the Committee agreed.

Reported in the *Eastbourne Gazette* on 29 March, following a meeting of the Eastbourne Watch Committee, the Committee advised that they would offer extra equipment for Hampden Park. They also said they would supply a fire escape, a hose cart and 600ft of hose. They agreed to enrol four local men into the Eastbourne Fire Brigade who would serve in Hampton Park.

After the March meeting, a welcome addition for the Eastbourne Fire Brigade was a new Merryweather "Greenwich" pattern telescopic fire escape ladder. When fully extended it reaches 40ft and has a box that can hold 600ft of hose and miscellaneous gear. They purchased this in July 1911.

In January 1912, Pevensey formed the Pevensey Fire Brigade with Mr J. H. Anderson as their captain, and he requested Captain Hounsom to instruct the twelve new members on their duties. There were also negotiations with the Eastbourne Corporation about buying one of their Manual fire engines. Mr C. Allen of Pevensey Mint House reached an agreement with the Corporation on the 24th January. He arranged for repairs to the Shand Mason appliance, and when completed, in mid-May, they delivered the engine to the Pevensey Fire Brigade. The licensee of the New Inn (now the Smugglers) offered to temporarily store the engine in the coach house behind the Inn. They stayed at these premises until a new engine house was built in September 1920.

Peter Winter

Not long after, Eastbourne bought their first motor fire engine. This was ordered in March and was a Leyland Motor Pump and Escape Appliance costing £925. It had a four-litre engine driving a water pump with a capacity of 400 gallons per minute. The water jet it produced could reach a height of 150 feet. *(Engine surplus to requirements in 1937)*. It had acetylene gas headlights with oil tail, side and ancillary lamps and carried a 50ft wheeled fire escape. This, and some old horse-drawn steam fire engines (one pre-1883 and the other 1889) and hand-drawn wheeled escapes and hose reels, were the total equipment available in Eastbourne until 1924.

They brought a matter up in the Council meeting in early September 1913, after a fire incident that occurred outside of the borough. The brigade reported they could not get horses from Messrs Chapman & Sons and had to assign the Leyland motor fire engine. The fire was at Friston, and close to Friston Place, so the Eastbourne Brigade responded. Back in November 1911, there had been a considerable barn fire in Friston Place. The Eastbourne Brigade had fought that fire for over twenty-four hours and estimated the damage to have been £1,000.

The Committee suggested that they should make the usual charge for attending the fire at Friston and in future, they should not take the motor fire engine outside of the borough. They also said they would review the terms for the supply of horses attending both inside and outside the borough. Then they decided they should leave the option to travel to fires outside of the borough to the discretion of the captain of the fire brigade.

In May 1914 the local paper reported that the Watch Committee had been advised that the Sick Fund for the fire brigade was "very much depleted". They suggested that at the next meeting of the Committee, they should consider a grant for the fund. They also noted that it had recently taken half an hour to find horses for the fire engine and one councillor suggested that two horses should always be ready to go to fires.

Captain Hounsom presented his annual report stating that there were no reports of serious fires in the past year and that property damage amounted to £1,265. He said only two members of his brigade held St John Ambulance certificates, whereas most police officers held them.

Whilst cycling near Seaford on 16 August, Fireman George Winchester, aged 38 years suddenly collapsed and died. His coffin, draped with purple and white, was carried to St. John's Church on the Steamer 'Morrison'. Captain Hounsom and thirty-four members of the Eastbourne Brigade were in attendance. There were also representatives from the Hailsham, Herstmonceux and Pevensey Fire Brigades. The Eastbourne Police lead the cortège and they buried him in Ocklynge Cemetery.

With WW1 raging, they called many men up for service, and the fire service was no exception. In March 1916, Captain Hounsom placed an advert in the *Eastbourne Gazette* asking for any active men over the age of forty-one to join the fire service. This could be temporary. He asked old members that had left the service to consider re-joining. At a military service tribunal on 5 April, Captain Hounsom applied for an exemption to military service for five members of the brigade. When asked, he stated that he had sixteen men of military age in the brigade. Fifteen men had joined the Forces, and now he only had forty men. His usual strength would be forty-six men. He advised them there were five fire stations, a motor fire engine, two Steamers plus six fire escapes and five hose carts.

He needed men to operate these. Then he told the tribunal that permanent firemen were exempt from service and we should keep the strength of the fire service up to protect the town. The tribunal granted a two-month postponement of their decision to enable Captain Hounsom to find further recruits.

There was not a sympathetic response to the March appeal, and the Watch Committee requested that Captain Hounsom should repeat it. The new notice appeared in the 12th April edition of the *Eastbourne Gazette*. A few days later, another advert was placed in the newspaper for a driver/engineer. Eight

COUNTY BOROUGH OF EASTBOURNE.

A GOOD PRACTICAL MOTOR ENGINEER and Driver wanted at once to drive and take charge (under the direction of the Chief Officer of the Fire Brigade) of a Motor Fire Engine, and to make himself generally useful and keep the Fire Station and Appliances clean. Wages 37s. 6d. per week with uniform, house, light and fuel. Apply, with reference to the Town Clerk, Town Hall, Eastbourne, not later than 29th April, 1916.

E/B Gazette 19 April 1916

applicants replied to the advertisement, and in June, the Watch Committee appointed Fireman A. Eldridge to this position.

Reported in May, at the Watch Committee meeting, was a letter from the Eastbourne Volunteer Training Corps. It listed the allocation and details of forty-five men sent to various local fire stations. They sent a copy to the captain of the fire brigade.

On Sunday evening at about 6.45 p.m. the 18 March 1917, passers-by discovered a fire in a boarding house in Lascelles Terrace. The residents in the house were all women who escaped except for an elderly and invalided woman, Miss Hill, aged 84 years. Mr Diplock was walking past the building on his way to Devonshire Park when the fire alarm was given. He was the Reel Foreman at Meads Fire Station and at once went to help. Five times Mr Diplock entered the burning smoke-filled building trying to find the woman and rescue her. The black suffocating smoke was hampering his search.

He borrowed a torch lamp from Mr H. Briggs, a special constable who also had entered the building and at last, they found the lady in a second-floor bedroom. She was not in bed but curled up in a chair in the room's corner between the bed and a cupboard. Then they both brought the lady out of the house. This all happened before the fire brigade engines had arrived. The brigade had received the alarm at 6.47 and arrived in Lascelles Terrace ten minutes later. They quickly extinguished the fire with their motor fire engine and hoses. Miss Hill was taken to hospital with cuts and slight burns but died later on Monday morning. At the inquest, they recorded a verdict of "Accidental Death" and stated that she died from shock.

Mr Diplock (aged 64 and affectionately known as "Dippy") had been an instructor at the Devonshire Park Baths for the last 33 years. He had already served twenty years in the brigade and received a long service medal and three bars. For his effort in March, they invited him to a reception. They held this at the Winter Gardens, Devonshire Park on Wednesday 13 June, where hundreds of people attended. The Society for the Protection of Life from Fire awarded him a silver medal and the Mayor, Alderman C. O'Brian, presented him with his award.

Also, in June, Captain Hounsom was still fighting with the Tribunal for exceptions for his men. He only had four men of military age and needed active men in the brigade. Other members of the service were five men aged between 60 and 65. Three aged between 55 and 60 and three between the ages of 45 and 55. The rest of his men were near the age of 41. The tribunal refused one application and granted a further twelve weeks of exception for the others.

One of the most destructive fires to occur in the town for many years was early on Saturday, 8 December. Just after 5.30 a.m., a passer-by discovered a fire at the premises of Messrs Noakes & Co in West Street. This company had an extensive turnery and steam joinery business. The police and fire brigade were at once notified of the fire and advised that there was a petrol store immediately in the vicinity. Captain Hounsom and his men rushed to the scene and ordered the removal of the petrol from the stores together with horses from a nearby stable. The flames had secured such a firm hold on the property that all the brigade could do, was direct their resources to protect neighbouring properties. The fire gutted the workshops, with just the walls remaining. There was valuable machinery strewn around and a large quantity of timber destroyed in the blaze.

The only other building to receive any damage was the business of Messrs A. H. Johnson & Co., a carriage builder. A few days later, the directors of Noakes & Co sent a letter to the editor of the *Eastbourne Gazette*. They thanked the fire service and police for their valiant efforts in tackling the fire. They also thanked Mr J. W. Woolnough and Messrs Mark Martin & Son. Who offered space and machinery on their premises so that they could carry on with their urgent war work.

In January 1918, the tribunal granted a twelve-week extension to Fireman Kenward, aged 41, to carry out his work as a fireman and dairy roundsman.

Special Constable Horton whilst passing the Beach Sanitary Laundry Co. on Royal Parade East on Wednesday 15 May, noticed smoke coming from the premises. He hurried to Latimer Road Police Station to raise the alarm. The fire brigade received the call at 12.50 a.m., and within ten minutes, the motor engine was at the scene. Members of Grove Road and Cavendish Place stations with Captain Hounsom in charge found the premises ablaze. The roof was about to collapse, and Captain Hounsom was told that employees had removed three motor vans and a horse to safety. The engineer at the laundry Mr H. J. Munday, who lives in property adjoining the laundry, had arranged the removal of the horse and vans.

With an ample supply and pressure of water, seven or eight lines of hose were soon playing on the flames. The firemen could not save the laundry building but turned their attention to Mr Munday's house. It was not until 3.15 a.m. that the fire was under control, but it had gutted the laundry building with just the skeleton walls remaining. All the washing received at the weekend was lost. The firemen could not find the cause of the fire, but they believed it to have started near or in the ironing room. Although insured, they estimate the damage at £5,000. This would not be the last large fire to affect a laundry business in Eastbourne.

In November, in recognition of Captain Hounsom's forty-year service, and his twenty-one years serving as their Captain, the brigade held a ceremony. This was at the fire station at Grove Road where members of the brigade presented him with a silver-plated tray.

18 July 1920, Eastbourne hosted the National Fire Brigades' Association competition when over fifty fire brigades from around the country descended on the town. They encamped at Summerdown Camp, and the events took place in Gildredge Park. Large crowds gathered during the week to watch displays and special attractions. Most of the displays were free to the public.

The major competitions took place on Thursday with motor pump, steamer, hose cart and escape competitive events. There was a fire pageant arranged by Mr Hounsom, Captain of the Eastbourne Brigade, showing the evolution of the fire engine.

First in line, was the double-handed 1823 appliance closely followed by a Manual, a Steamer and then the latest Eastbourne motor engine.

They reported in the *Eastbourne Herald* on 10 September 1921 that Mr Somerville J. Weakford died. Aged 72, he had served in the Eastbourne fire service, the last 23 years as an engineer in charge at Cavendish Place fire station. He was one of the original members of the private brigade organised by Mr Thomas Fuller.

Early on Sunday morning 30 October 1921, a fire broke out at the Endcliffe School in the Meads. This was only a small fire, and the firemen quickly extinguished it with chemical appliances. As a reward for the prompt attendance and help, the principal of the school, Miss Raymond, invited the brigade to the school dining-room. After sitting down, the school staff treated the firefighters to an early morning breakfast of steak and kidney pie, pastries, biscuits and coffee. It is nice to be appreciated.

Hampden Park fire station needed extra space, and in November tenders were sought for the building of a fire escape shed.

The Borough engineer placed adverts in the local newspapers inviting tenders for the work. The Committee received eight tenders, and they accepted the one from Mr Mark Hookham at £79 10s.

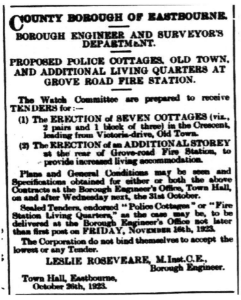

E/B Chronicle 27 October 1923

In 1923, there were discussions in the council regarding extra housing for appliances and firefighters. They required additional space at the Grove Road fire station. The Committee instructed the Borough Surveyor's department to place an advert in the *Eastbourne Chronicle*, which he did on the 27 October when he invited tenders for the erection of an additional storey to the building. This would provide increased living accommodation for the men. But it would take many years before they would draw up plans.

There was a fire reported in a building in Arundel Road and on the way to the blaze, the Leyland motor fire engine broke a back axle. The brigade needed a second engine, and in 1924 the Borough agreed to buy one. It was a Dennis Braidwood motor pump with a 50ft escape ladder supplied by Messrs Dennis Bros. Ltd, of Guildford. This engine had recently been on exhibition at the National Fire Brigades Camp at Oxford and cost the council £1,622. In 1951 the council sold this engine for £75.

In August, they tested the new Dennis 50/60 hp motor turbine engine. First, they drove it around the town on several hill-climbing tests. The engine successfully navigated Granville Hill, East Dean Hill and lastly Friston Hill, then on Wednesday 27 August at 3 o'clock, the brigade proceeded along King Edward's Parade by the Grand Hotel.

Joining them were the appliance from Compton Place and a rare outing of the original 1823 hand pump, manned by the Sea Cadets. Engineer Eldridge drove the 1912 Leyland motor appliance. The horse-drawn Steamers, 'Morrison' and 'Fire King' were also in attendance. Then they detached the escape ladders from their engines and placed them against the front of the Lansdowne Private Hotel. The ladder from the Dennis engine reached the top balcony, and the one from the Leyland reached the roof. The pressure from the 12-inch main was 70lb. They moved to the Town Hall and carried out a 'high lift' test. A jet of water was thrown over the top of the dome of the building. The new engine has a water capacity of 400 to 500 gallons.

Hundreds of spectators came out to watch the display and followed the engines to the Town Hall. Forty of the forty-seven members of the brigade under the command of their Captain, J. A. Hounsom were on duty together with Mr Harding, a representative from Messrs. Dennis Bros. Before the demonstration the firemen were inspected by the Mayor, Alderman G. Soddy. He then presented long service medals to Hose-reel Foreman Clifford Vernon and Fireman H. Payne. Both had completed 10 years' service as firemen. After the display, the firemen went to Grove Road station for tea and speeches from the Mayor and Mr Harding.

Early December the brigade attended the funeral of a long serving fireman, Sub-Engineer John W. Hudson. The service was held at the Central Wesleyan Church and the interment took place at Ocklynge Cemetery.

There was a social gathering on Monday 24 January 1927 of the Eastbourne Fire Brigade. This was to celebrate Captain J. A. Hounsom's 70th birthday. There were tributes of appreciation from the Mayor, Alderman Soddy and other members of the council thanking him for his extended service in the brigade. And his work with the national bodies of the fire service. Captain Hounsom has been connected with the fire service for forty-five years, from the days of a small hand-drawn engine, and a single fire escape to today's pair of motor engines and many hose reels and escapes.

Uniforms always needed replacement because of damage or for recruits and in February 1927 the Committee accepted a tender from Messrs. Huggins, Son & Co to supply extra uniforms. They quoted cloth suits at 73s 5d, overcoats at 58s 6d and caps at 8s 6d. At the meeting, they discussed the matter of repairs needed to the roof of the Grove Road fire station. It was also noted that the electric showroom was going to move offices. The brigade requested to take back the space they had occupied as they wanted to house an additional fire engine and said they would need extra quarters for one or two men. In reply, the Committee said they were still discussing the matter.

At the March meeting of the Watch Standing Sub-Committee, they agreed that the Borough Surveyor would draw up plans.

These would be for the alterations to the electric showroom and plans for extra accommodation for one or two men. They also accepted a quotation from Dennis Bros Ltd for four exhaust and four inlet valves for the Dennis fire engine. The cost of these would be £5 5sh.

Robert Francis

February 1926 the EFB dinner dance at Devonshire Park.

In April, Sub-Engineer Morant sustained an injury during a drill and was taken off duty and put on the sick list for ten days. It was agreed by the Committee that the Brigade would pay his doctor's bill.

The Borough Surveyor in May submitted three plans and estimates to the Committee. These were for the alterations to the fire station. Later in October he supplied amended plans for the extra accommodation and the addition of a Mansard roof as they had requested. The estimated costs would be £1,600 for the alterations plus work to the electricity showroom at £650, Totalling £2,250. The Watch Committee accepted the costs.

The equipment which the brigade had at this time was two motor engines, a Steamer, five escapes and hose carts.

In September 1927, as the parish was looking forward to celebrating its golden jubilee, tragedy struck when fire gutted All Saints' Church in Carlisle Road.

It reduced the inside of the church to a mass of charred and twisted wreckage, leaving only the tower and the outside shell.

In the early evening of Thursday 29th, some residents noticed smoke coming from the church. This did not bother them as they thought this was just emitting from the chimneys. Sometime later Mrs Hanks, the vicar's wife, when she went outside, noticed there was smoke billowing from the roof at the eastern side. She immediately telephoned the fire brigade.

The brigade received the call at about 5.40 p.m. and called thirty men out from the Central station, Cavendish Place, Meads and Old Town. They did not request crews from Hampden Park. The first appliance with Engineer Eldridge in charge was on scene within 4½ minutes, and they attached hoses to hydrants. They took two deliveries from the pump, which they focused on the roof of the church. Two engines were in attendance at the church, but they only used one. At 8 p.m., they sent one engine back to the fire station, and the other remained until 9.30. Six firemen were left on duty all night. At 1 a.m., they were still attending to outbursts of fires by the North wall. This was a difficult fire and had taken hold well before they called the brigade.

It had been a pelting with rain, with the wind blowing furiously, the fire crews could do very little to save the roof. But they protected the two vestries and the tower. The fire destroyed the interior of the main building together with the church organ. They had recently refurbished the organ at a cost of several hundred pounds, and it was a memorial to the church's first Vicar. The fire also destroyed twenty stained glass windows. The estimated damage to the property was between £25,000 and £30,000. Captain Hounsom did not attend the blaze as he had departed that morning to the Fire Brigades' Autumn Conference in Leeds.

The cost of replacing the church would be thousands of pounds. With designs from A.R.G. Fenning and P.D. Stonham, they soon brought plans forward for a new building. In June 1929 they held the first service in the renovated church.

A few days before Christmas on the 19th December, the fire service received a call to a blaze in Upper Dicker where part of the Tudor wing of Michelham Priory was on fire. It was a bitterly chilly night, and the Eastbourne crews joined Hailsham and Lewes firefighters to control the fire. Because of a delay in calling the fire service, the west wing was burning fiercely when firefighters arrived. When they arrived at the Priory, they had to break the ice in the moat to secure sufficient water supply. The firemen were drenched with water that froze on their uniforms and some of their hoses also froze. It was early afternoon when the firefighters completely extinguished the blaze and when the brigade was packing up to leave, they discovered their hoses were frozen. They could not roll up the hoses for the journey back to Eastbourne. They had to lay them out like scaffold poles on the hose cart.

The Priory is owned by Mr R. B. Wright. He purchased it 2½ years previously and was renovating the building. It was the Tudor wing of the Priory that suffered severe damage.

Fireman Quincey in January 1928 whilst taking part in a drill with the fire escape, broke his wrist. The escape unit was now thirty-two years old, and the captain of the fire brigade considered it unsafe. He requested they should purchase a new one at an estimated cost of £200. After the Committee had received tenders, they decided at the May/July meetings to accept the lowest bid. Merryweather & Sons were successful and agreed to supply a 65ft fire escape that would cost £249 10sh.

East Dean and Friston Parish Council in April requested the terms that Eastbourne Fire Brigade required to attend fires in their Parish. They quoted the Parish Fire Engine Act 1898 and wished to start discussions with Eastbourne Borough. The Fire Sub-Committee decided they would not recommend the Council to enter into any agreement.

An article appeared in the *Eastbourne Chronicle* in May 1928. This was part of a series of articles named "While Eastbourne Sleeps". This particular writing, number six in the series was about a night at the fire station. It explained that two retained firemen were on duty from seven until ten each evening. When they finish their shifts, they switch the alarms upstairs to the quarters of the permanent men. Either Engineer Albert Eldridge or one of his colleagues always sleep at the station ready to receive any alarm. When they receive a call, the fireman will find out where it is and push the main button. This will set off thirty bells in the houses of sleeping firemen. He then will go downstairs and start the fire engine ready for the men who are hurrying to the station. Then he advises the Chief Fire Officer. When the main push is activated, it also advises Cavendish Place fire station. They then make a telephone call to Meads and Old Town stations.

The first fire crews on the scene quickly assess the blaze and will either ask other stations to "Come On" or "Stop". If the "Come On" call is made, then all stations must attend the fire. Sometimes they are asked to "Come along and look at a fire". It that case the duty officer rings a 'circuit bell' which calls out four men. They will stay on duty in the fire station until advised they are no longer required or have to set off with the fire engine. The fire engines will usually leave within four minutes of receiving a call. The first fireman to respond to the call and arrive at the fire station will take the Brigade's car. He will then drive to the Captain's house and convey him to the scene of the fire.

At the previous May meeting, the Committee requested the Borough Surveyor to readvertise for tenders for the additional works on the Grove Road fire station. This appeared in the *Eastbourne Chronicle* in early September.

By late September they had received four tenders with the lowest of these from Messrs Miller & Selmes Ltd of Pevensey Road. Their tender was for £2,500 and the Committee accepted this subject to sureties being satisfactory. It would be some years before they commenced work on the fire station.

Hailsham and Eastbourne had always had a friendly relationship and co-operated with each other. So, when Eastbourne received a call on 19 December for assistance. They responded immediately, driving eight miles through thick fog to reach Hailsham. There was an extensive fire in Hailsham High Street, and the local brigade was having trouble controlling it.

COUNTY BOROUGH OF EASTBOURNE.

BOROUGH ENGINEER'S DEPARTMENT.

Proposed Alterations & Additions to Grove Road Fire Station.

The Watch Committee are prepared to receive TENDERS for alterations and additions to the Grove Road Fire Station.

Plans, Specifications, and form of tender may be obtained, and contract may be seen, at the Borough Engineer's Office, Town Hall, Eastbourne, on payment of a deposit of One Guinea, which will be refunded on receipt of a bona-fide Tender and return of plans and specifications.

Sealed tenders endorsed "Grove Road Fire Station" to be delivered at the Borough Engineer's Office, not later than first post on Friday, the 21st September, 1928.

The lowest or any Tender will not necessarily be accepted.

By Order.

LESLIE ROSEVEARE, C.Inst. C.E.,
Borough Engineer & Surveyor.

Town Hall, Eastbourne.
3rd September, 1928.

A cycle repair shop above a wireless shop belonging to Messrs A. F. Smith Ltd had caught fire. Bert Arnott who worked in the wireless shop discovered the blaze a little before 4.30 in the afternoon. Although the local brigade captained by Mr Chapman was situated just along the High Street, by the time they arrived on the scene and fixed their hoses, the flames were shooting fifteen to twenty feet into the air.

The pressure of the water from the hydrants was low and had little effect in dousing the flames. Hailsham's appliance could not cope with the inferno, so requested help. Most of the adjoining shops were now in danger of severe damage from the fire. Eastbourne's engine arrived a little after 5 o'clock and being more powerful and carrying more hoses by 5.50 had the blaze under control. They had run hoses 100 yards at the rear of the buildings and utilised three nearby ponds. Then they poured two powerful jets of water on to the blaze. They then moved to the front of the premises and attacked the fire. At this time the roof of the shop collapsed followed shortly after by the shop window of the wireless store failing out onto the pavement. The fire destroyed two shops fronting the main street. This was the worst fire in living memory in the town, and they estimated the damage at £3,000.

The Council held a grand reception on 28 January 1929 in the Mayor's Parlour at the Town Hall. This was to honour Captain Hounsom for completing fifty years as a fireman in the Eastbourne Fire Brigade and thirty-one years as their Chief Fire Officer. The Mayor (Colonel Roland Gwynne) presented him with a chiming bracket clock. In acknowledgement, Captain Hounsom recalled that when he first joined, the town only had a Manual appliance. Now he said the town has two motor engines, six escapes, four hose carts and five fire stations.

But it was time for an additional appliance. He suggested they should buy a foam thrower, for dealing with the risk of petrol fires. The brigade was entirely staffed by volunteers, except for two permanent firemen. The first appointed in 1912 and the other in 1919. There were forty-seven firemen in service. Except for the disastrous fire at All Saints' Church, the average losses from fires did not exceed £500 per annum. The cost to the town at present for the fire service was £2,800 per year.

The Duke and Duchess of York visited Eastbourne for the first time on Tuesday 29 October. Local dignitaries greeted them at the railway station. The visit was to celebrate the purchase by the Council of a large stretch of the Downs. An area from Beachy Head through to Folkington, some 4,000 acres of land. The royal couple arrived by train drawn by the King Arthur class "Sir Balin" steam engine. At the end of Gildredge Road, firemen erected two escapes and formed an arch. This was 45ft high and manned by some of the crew. Below between two motor engines, they set up hoses and a fountain of water sent a spray into the air. This produced a gushing fountain that entertained the visitors and waiting crowds of onlookers.

First, the royal visitors were driven to the Town Hall, where they were officially greeted with speeches from the Mayor and then a reply from the Duke. Then they departed to Memorial Square and the War Memorial, where they laid a wreath. And then on to Beachy Head, where they unveiled two memorial seats before being taken for lunch at the Grand Hotel.

E/B Chronicle 2 November 1929

The fisherman had erected an arch in front of the Albion Hotel. They decorated this with fishing nets, oars and lifebelts. As the Duke passed the fireman's arch on the way to the railway station for his return journey to London, they rang the fire bells on the engines. The royal visitors departed Eastbourne at 4.20 p.m.

The *Eastbourne Chronicle* on 28 December 1929 reported a diamond jubilee celebration for Old Town fireman Mr Fred Newman. He first joined the Eastbourne fire service, aged 12, as a messenger and became a fireman when he was 15 years old. For many years Mr Newman has been Engineer-in-charge at the Old Town fire station and had just completed 60 years in the Eastbourne Fire Brigade. The family has strong connections with the fire service, and the Newman family are well known in Old Town. Councillor William Newman served with the brigade, and one of Fred's cousins also served. Another cousin Albert is still in the brigade with over 20 years' service.

Mr Fred Newman's sons Fred and Walter are serving fireman, and his son-in-law was once in the brigade.

Armistice Day November 1918
To the left of Capt. Hounsom, Driving, is Albert Eldridge, to his left standing is Fm. Steve Gausden

Many thanks to the Eldridge Family for the copy of this Picture

Robert Sumsion

Carnival Time

Michael Garrett

30 August 1924 Engine trial along seafront.

Michael Garrett

5 REORGANISATION

Captain Hounsom advised the Watch Committee in January 1930 that he wanted smoke helmets supplied to his men. The Committee discussed this. They asked him if he could arrange for a demonstration of the helmets and a foam generator. He also suggested they buy a twin generator, a tender and cartridges costing about £350. They agreed to consider the idea.

With the population rapidly growing, Hampden Park only had a small fire sub-station. In January there was a discussion in the local newspaper about the equipment they used at the local fire station. They mentioned that the Fire Chief was requesting the supply of up-to-date appliances for the Eastbourne Brigade. The journalist considered that Hampden Park had antiquated equipment and should be more of a priority for the Committee. He suggested that it was time they stationed a motor pump in Hampden Park.

The National Fire Brigades' Association Widows' and Orphans' Fund offers a prize to the brigade that raises the most funds in a year. After much fund-raising, Eastbourne won this in March 1930, for collecting £217 and received a shield as their award. The town had previously won the shield in 1907 and 1927, beating brigades from all over England and Wales. Lord Ampthill presented the shield to Captain Hounsom at a Holborn restaurant in London.

They decided at the Watch Standing Sub-Committee after much discussion they needed to reorganise the Eastbourne fire service. They agreed they should consult with the Chief Fire Officer of the London Brigade; Mr A. R. Dye. He could inspect the brigade and recommend how they could restructure the service. This would undoubtedly bring radical changes.

In January, the *Eastbourne Chronicle* reported that the Watch Committee and Town Council have accepted the report from Mr Dyer and were considering adjustments to update their local fire service.

In his report, he suggested that in the future, the service ought to include full-time men with a Chief Officer. There should be residential quarters available at the Central fire station in Grove Road. The firemen should carry out regular pressure tests on the hoses and they should reduce crews from forty volunteer firemen to twenty full-time men. Also, they should drill the men more often than they had been in earlier years. The report criticised the number of fire call boxes available and advised that they needed more.

They should place them in town a quarter of a mile from each other. It was also suggested they should close the sub-stations at Hampden Park, Old Town and Meads.

The London County Council did not charge a fee for the inspection and only asked for out-of-pocket expenses. But the Watch Committee offered ten guineas to Chief Officer Dye for his valued help. After receiving the report, the Watch Committee wanted to modernise the fire service.

With the new changes about to happen, Captain Hounsom decided to resign his position. But he agreed to stay until they found a replacement. The council then decided they should create a professional position of Chief Fire Officer. They appointed Mr Douglas W. Spence. He had served in the First World War with the Royal Army Service Corps, which provided fire protection services for the army. In 1919 aged 24, he joined the London Fire Brigade. This was at the Whitechapel fire station. He moved to Kent in March 1928 and became Second Officer of Tonbridge Fire Brigade. In January 1930, he joined Watford Fire Brigade as their Chief Fire Officer.

Members of the fire brigade made a presentation to Captain Hounsom in recognition of his many years of service. They held this on Saturday night, 29 March 1931, with a well-attended farewell supper in the Grove Road Fire Station. On behalf of his fellow firemen, Chief Engineer Eldridge presented Captain Hounsom with a case of pipes, cigars, tobacco and a smoker's knife.

On the night of Monday 30 March, Hailsham Brigade called the Eastbourne Brigade for assistance. A fierce fire had broken out in the premises of Green Bros, and the Hailsham men were having trouble dealing with it. There was a lack of sufficient water, and within an hour and a half, the fire destroyed the factory. A blow for the town of Hailsham as this rendered thirty to forty workmen without employment.

Local dog breeder and architectural woodcarver, Mr Frederick G. Richards, suffered a second disastrous fire on Christmas morning at his workshop in Ashford Road. A neighbour, Miss Kathleen Sturgis, discovered the fire at six o'clock in the morning and informed another neighbour, Mr Frederick Foord, who then called the brigade. Mr Richards was a dog breeder of bull terriers and lost one of these and a fox terrier in the blaze. The brigade received the call at six minutes past six and despatched the Dennis fire appliance with an escape. Three minutes later, the Leyland fire engine with twelve auxiliary men followed and within twenty minutes they brought the fire under control. Firefighters were on scene until mid-day to protect against further ignition.

Whilst fighting the fire, Fireman Frank Taylor injured his left hand carrying a dog to safety when he partly fell through a hole in the floor. His bulky breathing apparatus saved him from falling through the floorboards. They took him for treatment, and his injury required four stitches at the Princess Alice Hospital.

There had been a previous fire at Mr Richard's workshop in February when three bull terriers lost their lives. At that fire, one of the crew Fireman Payne also received an injury. He had to take time off work, and in May 1931, the Town Council agreed to pay him an additional compassionate allowance.

With the reorganisation, there would be changes and, at a meeting of the Watch Committee in June 1931, they decided that older members of the brigade should retire. The Town Clerk sent letters to the men advising them of these recent changes to the way the service would work. The committee agreed to hold a presentation at the Town Council, where the retiring members would receive certificates "recording the very sincere appreciation of the Town Council". They arranged for this to take place on the 5th of August.

COUNTY BOROUGH OF EASTBOURNE.

FIRE BRIGADE.

Applications are invited for the position of Driver Fireman. Preference will be given to a man with engineering experience. The wages will be £2/10/0 per week with free living accommodation, fuel, light and uniform. The appointment will be subject to the provisions of the Fire Brigades' Pension Act, 1925, and the selected candidate will be required to pass a medical examination.

Applications accompanied by not more than three recent testimonials, should be forwarded to the Fire Brigade Chief Officer, Grove Road, Eastbourne, not later than SATURDAY, 4th July. Envelopes to be endorsed "Driver Fireman."

DOUGLAS W. SPENCE,
Chief Officer.

E/B Chronicle 27 June 1931

Since their last meeting, the brigade had purchased extra equipment. This included hook ladders, 'Proto' breathing apparatus, and new hand control branches. The new branches enabled firefighters to control the flow of water onto a fire.

Whilst Chief Officer Spence was in Hampden Park in December, they called him to an incident in a house in Percival Road. When he arrived at the building, it was blazing furiously. The engines from Eastbourne were on their way. Local crews used chemical extinguishers until the first engine from the Central station arrived with its first-aid appliance that could connect to a hydrant. They soon brought the fire under control. But the fireman had to use two sets of breathing apparatus for them to safely reach the first floor. Mr Spence was in Hampden Park to oversee the installation of three new fire alarms. These were in Elm Grove, and the junctions of Rosebery Avenue, and Neville Road, and at the junction of Lottbridge Drove and Kingston Road.

After a recent fire in a flat at South Cliff in January 1932, the owner Mr M. D. Horn donated to the firemen's recreation fund. This was in appreciation of their services, and he gave this to Chief Fire Officer Spence. The brigade received the call at 5.31 p.m. and despatched two engines. They extinguished the fire within ten minutes. After an investigation, they concluded that coal falling from the fireplace onto the carpet caused the incident. A few days later, on the 15 January, the brigade received a call to a fire in a confectioner's shop in Seaside. Again, this was not a serious fire, but the firefighters had to use three sets of breathing apparatus because of the excessive smoke. Two fire engines and fifteen men attended this blaze, which they brought under control in twenty minutes.

Finally, they made alterations to the Grove Road fire station in 1932 when they removed the roof and added an extra floor to the building. This gave a further seven rooms, and they opened a third bay to house an engine in the old electricity showrooms. The top floor was used as a residential home for the Chief Fire Officer and his family.

The 1912 Leyland appliance had passed its prime, and the Leyland Motor Company quoted £282 to recondition the engine. This motor had solid wheels and they could not convert them to pneumatic tyres. The Committee presented plans to the Council in February 1932, who approved the purchase of a new motor turntable ladder. Together with an escape van, new hoses and hook ladders. They also agreed to alterations to the Central Fire Station and the addition of three permanent firemen posts. The costs for the equipment and men's wages amounted to £4,475. They also arranged to buy a Merryweather wooden 100ft four-section turntable ladder. This appliance was on solid tyres, and later they organised the fitting of pneumatic tyres.

The Chief Fire Officer gave an interview to the *Eastbourne Gazette*, which appeared in the 24 February edition. In it, he discussed some operations of the fire service. He first explained to the public how the fire alarm system worked. Then he stated how important it was for everyone to contact the fire service the moment they discovered fire. The switchboard was the nerve centre for all the alarms around the town.

The Central Fire Station receives calls whether from fire alarm boxes or by telephone. Within minutes and usually, before the bell has stopped ringing, the first engine would be ready to go. The second engine would be ready shortly afterwards.

They record all calls on a tape machine. When they receive a telephone call from Hampden Park about a fire, the duty officer turns a handle on the switchboard and tells the sub-station. Should the fire alarm box be activated in Hampden Park, then an alarm is sent simultaneously to the sub-station and Grove Road.

Chief Officer Spence stated that no matter how small the fire, the brigade always responds to the call. Also, they fit all their appliances with first-aid boxes. He said that if the fire was a chimney or hearth fire, he would like the public to inform them. As then, they would only dispatch one engine. As a note of interest, if you see the firemen wearing their cloth caps, then they are attending a chimney fire.

In May, Eastbourne took delivery of a new Merryweather (Dorman) fire engine. This had a 6 cylinder 90 hp engine and 100ft turntable ladder. This engine had been sold to many brigades throughout the country and cost the Borough £2,975.

At the October meeting of the Watch Committee, there was some disquiet. This was about the alleged preferential treatment given to the fire service. Some council members were not happy that the wages for the firemen were £3 15s plus free quarters, fuel and light. The men also received free of charge uniforms, a pension and medical treatment. They thought this was too generous. The chairman responded by stating that the Finance Committee had given this question great thought. The Borough Treasurer, who based the scale of wages and allowances on similar schemes in force around the country, had carefully drawn these new arrangements up. We have not treated our firemen more generously than in other towns.

November saw the annual Eastbourne Fire Brigade's ball at the Winter Garden, held in aid of various Fire Brigade charities. Over 850 people attended with music supplied by Frank Arthur's Band and Norman Mellor and his dance orchestra. Seven firemen remained at the fire station on call, and a fire engine stood outside the Winter Garden throughout the evening in readiness should extra crews be needed. The dancing carried on until one a.m. Proceeds from the dance would go to the National and Professional Fire Brigade's Widows' and Orphans' Fund. During the current year, the Fund had paid grants totalling £104 to Eastbourne aged firemen and widows of firemen.

In January 1933, the Eastbourne Corporation and Eastbourne Rural District Council came to an understanding. This followed a meeting in October when Chief Fire Officer Spence brought to the Watch Committees attention the advice given by The National Fire Brigade Association.

He was referring to paragraph 4 in the Schedule of Charges which the Corporation had agreed to. The Rural Council now would contribute 1d of the rates to Eastbourne, and in return, the Eastbourne Fire Brigade would "be at the disposal of the Rural Council in case of fire". There would be no further charge to the owners and occupiers of properties. The Pevensey Fire Brigade would cover the Pevensey and Westham parish area. This agreement was for three years.

Robert Francis

Funeral of 31-year-old Fireman T. W. Harmer, 7th February 1933 at All Souls' Church.

The comradery in the fire service is very strong. It is a common practice for serving firemen to be joined by other members of their family, serving in the brigade. The bond between firefighters is very special, and through the ages, the tradition has carried on. Even today, sons follow their fathers into the fire service.

One such family in Eastbourne was that of William George Hunt. He entered the Brigade in 1895. During the Boar War, he left to fight with the Royal Sussex Regiment. But re-joined the fire service on his return. In 1921 one of his sons, also William George joined the Eastbourne Brigade. Another son, Cecil, later followed the family tradition and enlisted with the brigade.

On the previous page, all three members of the family are paying their respects at the funeral of former auxiliary Fireman Thomas. W. Harmer. They carried his coffin on Eastbourne's first motor engine, the 1912 Leyland Motor Pump. The service was conducted at All Souls' Church, and they buried him at Ocklynge Cemetery.

Other local families followed this tradition of serving in the Brigade; The Brooks, Diplock, Dowsett, Gausden, Gosden, Newman and Terry families are just some of them.

Robert Francis

William George Hunt Snr.

Robert Francis

William George Hunt.

Cecil Hunt.

The Watch Committee decided Cavendish Place fire station was no longer needed, so they agreed to lease the building. A local company took on the lease from 25 March 1933 for seven years at an agreed rent of £60 a year. After the formation of the National Fire Service in 1941, the Cavendish Place fire station opened again to help in the war effort.

In the early hours of Thursday 8 June, passers-by discovered a fire at the Royal Marine Laundry in Winchelsea Road and alerted the warehouse foreman, Mr King. The owners founded the company fifty years ago. And the company was one of the town's oldest laundries in Eastbourne employing ninety people. It was 6.35 a.m. when P.C. Clayton telephoned the police station who then informed the fire brigade. They at once dispatched the motor escape and within a few minutes, the motor ladders and motor pump followed. The firefighters surrounded the building, and with ten deliveries of water from the nearby yachting pond, and three hydrants, they had the blaze under control by 9 a.m. Although the inferno destroyed

EASTBOURNE CHRONICLE, SATURDAY, JUNE 10, 1933.

Another picture showing firemen among the debris at the destroyed premises of the Royal Marine Laundry.

the main building, the brigade stopped the fire reaching the wash-house and boiler room and the possibility of the boilers exploding.

The laundry catered for local schools and hotels, and they had cleaned and packed the premises with goods ready to return to their owners. Unfortunately, the fire destroyed all the customer's belongings. The building was in a residential part of town, and hundreds of spectators turned out to watch their local firemen at work. They watched the flames rising to a height of sixty feet from the building. The police were present and controlled the crowds.

The Eastbourne Rural Council held a meeting in March 1934 when they discussed a letter from the Jevington Parish Council advising that it was not common knowledge that the Eastbourne Fire Brigade service was available to their residents. The fact was that the fire service was available to all in the rural district.

They wanted to put up notices informing the public of this service. The Rural Council approved the idea, and they left it to the clerk to arrange this.

At the Town Council meeting in October, the Watch Committee proposed an increase in the car allowance for Chief Officer Spence.

They wanted it increased from £50 to £75, as he had suggested that running the car for brigade work was costing him £100 per year. They also suggested that Hailsham Rural District Council should contribute £35 per year towards Mr Spence's expenditure, as he was carrying out extensive duties in their area.

Later in October, the Council sold Meads Fire Station for £1,200 to William and Emily Gertrude Midson. Mr Midson then opened the premises as a motor garage. Expenses for the sale were £37 10s, and the Council would offset the nett balance of £1,162 10sh against the cost of the extension to the Grove Road fire station.

On the 9 March 1935, the Council invited tenders for alterations to the Grove Road fire station. They proposed to alter and raise the Hose Tower, and their advertisement stated that the "lowest tender will not necessarily be accepted". The following week Eastbourne Town Clerk placed an advert in the *Eastbourne Gazette*. It invited tenders for a new Closed-in Pattern Fire Engine. They wanted a new engine, and the advert stated that "it must come equipped with a comprehensive range of accessories".

COUNTY BOROUGH OF EASTBOURNE.

PROPOSED ALTERATIONS TO HOSE AND DRILL TOWER AT FIRE BRIGADE STATION.

TENDERS are invited for the raising and altering of the Hose Tower at the Fire Brigade Station. Grove Road. Eastbourne.

Plans and General Conditions may be seen and Specification and Tender Form obtained from the Borough Engineer's Office. Town Hall.

No Tender will be considered unless it is sent in a plain sealed envelope addressed to the Town Clerk bearing the words "TENDER FOR HOSE TOWER ALTERATIONS" but shall not bear any name or mark indicating the sender.

Tenders must be received not later than 12 noon on Thursday. March 21st. 1935.

The lowest or any tender will not necessarily be accepted.

H. W. POVARGUE.
Town Clerk.

Town Hall. Eastbourne.
9th March. 1935.

E/B Gazette 13 March 1935

COUNTY BOROUGH OF EASTBOURNE.

FIRE ENGINE.

THE Council invite Tenders for the supply of a Closed-in Pattern Fire Engine, with a comprehensive range of accessories.

Specifications may be obtained on application to the Chief Officer. Fire Station. Eastbourne. Tenders must be received not later than Friday. 31st May. 1935, and no tender will be considered unless it is sent in a plain sealed envelope addressed to the Town Clerk, bearing the words "Tender for Fire Engine" but shall not bear any name or mark indicating the sender. The lowest or any tender will not necessarily be accepted.

H. W. POVARGUE.
Town Clerk.

Town Hall.
Eastbourne.

E/B Gazette 24 April 1935

In June, the *Eastbourne Gazette* reported that Eastbourne firemen had once again won recognition. They received the Shield from the Brigade Association Widows' and Orphans' Fund for raising the most funds in the year 1934.

Early July at the meeting of the Town Council, the Mayor presented long service medals to two firemen.

RECEIVED FOR GIVING.—Eastbourne Fire Brigade with the shield they have just won for subscribing the largest amount to the Professional Fire Brigades' Association Widows' and Orphans' Fund for 1934.

E/B Gazette 5 June 1935

They were Auxiliary-Fireman Payne and Auxiliary-Fireman F. Gosden. Fireman Payne had joined the service in April 1914 at Cavendish Place fire station and except for a period on war service, has served continuously ever since. He has recently obtained his St John Ambulance certificate, and since January 1932, has attended 211 fire calls, and 179 drills and performed other duties at the fire station, each of three hours' duration. Fireman Gosden, who works for the Gas Company, joined the brigade in 1920 and served at Grove Road fire station. Since 1932 he had attended 219 fire calls, 180 drills and 113 duties at the fire station. He also qualified for St John ambulance work. They congratulated both men for their "excellent long service in helping others".

At a meeting of the Watch Committee in early October. Chief Officer Spence said that with approval from the Committee he would put on a public display. This would be on the first Tuesday of each month. They would carry out a demonstration of drills "for the benefit and instruction of the general public". The Committee gave their approval.

With the changes to Grove Road fire station, Chief Office Spence on an inspection of the building in November made an unusual find in the basement. He found an old fire appliance scattered around in pieces. This was an old manual engine dating back to the early 1800s. Carved into the woodwork at one end was the name "Bristow Fecit" and "308" at the other end. John Bristow from London used to make fire engines for Richard Newsham. And the design of the one found was similar to Newsham's design.

They gathered together all the parts, and the firemen reconstructed the old appliance.

When testing the engine, they noted that it could lift water to a height of fifty-six feet. This was probably the old Vestry machine, and they displayed it at the Grove Road station. The *Eastbourne Courier* carried the story in their 8 November edition. Years later in 1943, the fire station received a direct hit from a German bomb, which wrecked the engine.

ESRO

1935 Testing the old Vestry fire appliance.

In early January 1936, the brigade took delivery of a new covered fire engine. This was one of the most up-to-date machines available and was a complete emergency outfit. It carried a 35ft telescopic ladder with ancillary hook and scaling ladders. Another extra feature was that it had a canteen that could cater for six men, the driver and officer crew. They could also use the new appliance as an ambulance.

P.C. Powell, whilst on patrol, discovered a fire at the Elysium Cinema in Seaside and telephoned the fire brigade from a nearby police lodge. The cinema which can accommodate 800 is the third-largest in the town and received serious damage in the fire.

The fire started at 00.20 hrs on Tuesday 17 March and destroyed the screen, curtains, the organ and a grand piano. Chief Fire Officer Spence and Second Officer Phillips were quickly on the scene with three engines. They soon had five deliveries playing on the flames using about 1,000 ft of hose. One length was attached to a hydrant in Firle Road and taken into the cinema through an emergency exit and up through the auditorium. Then through a window and on to the roof and within two hours firefighters had the fire under control. The blaze was confined to the cinema and was prevented from spreading to neighbouring properties, including the Birkbeck Garage, Seaside and houses in Firle Road and Poplar Row.

Wednesday evening, the 8 April, a fire broke out at the premises of the Hampshire Tyre Company in Albert Parade. P.C. Pryce discovered the blaze and contacted the fire brigade at 9.45 p.m. With Chief Fire Officer Spence and Second Officer Phillips, they were on the scene within minutes. The fire had originated in the cellar, and dense black smoke was issuing into the building. Fireman had to wear breathing apparatus, but one, Fireman Taylor, was temporarily overcome before he could fit his equipment. Two first-aid jets and three hydrant deliveries were used together with two searchlights. After about an hour, the brigade had the fire under control. The basement and ground floor received considerable damage, as did the manager's flat on the first floor, which sustained damage from the heat and smoke.

An enormous fire broke out in Mark Lane on Monday evening, the 25th of May which they reported in the *Eastbourne Gazette*. By the time the brigade arrived on the scene at 7 p.m., the fire had taken hold, and smoke was billowing through the roof.

Second Officer Phillips was in charge of the brigade as Chief Fire Officer Spence was in Edinburgh. He was attending a conference of the Professional Fire Brigades' Association.

They brought three engines to attend the fire and five jets were playing into the flames, Hydrants from three roads were being used. The street was full of curious spectators whilst the firemen with their motor fire escape directed heavy jets of water onto the building. It was not until 9.45 p.m. that it was safe for the firemen to leave. The fire had consumed the warehouse of Messrs R. H. and J. Pearson Ltd, and they estimated the damage to run into thousands of pounds.

The firemen stopped the fire extending to nearby properties, and crews with breathing equipment entered the building to cut off the electricity and gas supplies. The main warehouse with large stocks of paint and other inflammable materials was on the first floor.

They saved the shops beneath the warehouse that belonged to boot repairer, Messrs T. & S. Piper, china riveter, Mr L. Butcherd, picture frame maker, Mr J. S. Stofer and electricians, Messrs Young & Co. But the shops suffered severe water damage. The following morning, the firemen were still in Mark Lane, damping down the remnants of the blaze.

Calais Fire Brigade's Chief Officer, M. Vigne, who in September, was staying in Hastings decided to visit Eastbourne. He wanted to visit the town's fire station and renew his acquaintance with Mr Spence. They had met last year when Mr Spence paid a visit to Calais. The French fire chief was very impressed with the Eastbourne fire station and whilst chatting the two fire chiefs discovered they were at school together in Brighton.

Members of the Eastbourne Fire Brigade (including Captain Younsom, third left back row) at their dinner on Saturday evening.

E/B Gazette 7 October 1936

85

On Saturday the 3rd October, the brigade attended the funeral of one of its own. Harry Diplock aged 76, and known to his friends as Dippy. 'Professor' Diplock had for fifty-four years been an instructor at the Devonshire Baths, helping many residents to learn to swim. Included with the 12,000 people he taught to swim were many notables including Princes, Princesses, the ex-King and Queen of Portugal as well as the Maharaja of Cooch Behar. He was also Reel Foreman at Cavendish Place fire station and had received a long service medal. They carried his coffin draped with the Union Jack on one of the fire engines to St. John's Church and the burial was at Ocklynge Cemetery. Firemen in dress uniform attended the cortège, and retired firemen were also in attendance.

Early morning on 17 Dec, the fire brigade received a call to a fire in the roof of the Cavendish Hotel. Because of the extreme weather and a severe gale, they could only extend their ladders 60ft. The firefighters had to carry their hoses through the hotel and up the main stairway; the blaze was extinguished within an hour, although water damaged some bedrooms. The hotel staff moved guests from their rooms into the lounge where they served tea and coffee.

Before the outbreak of war, the fire service was having difficulties recruiting new members. They advised the Watch Committee in February 1937 of the problems they were having filling its vacancies. Chief Officer Spence advised the Committee that only four applicants had replied to their advertisements to join the service. Two men were not eligible because of their age. One was not an experienced driver, and a third did not return his application form. The Chief Fire Officer suggested he would try to recruit men from His Majesty's Armed Forces. The Committee agreed.

A small fire occurred at Beal's timber yard in Hampden Park in early May. Damage to the premises was limited, but the brigade was once again held up at the level crossing.

To mark the King George VI coronation in May 1937, the town planned a week of celebrations. One event to take place on Wednesday afternoon was the Historical Procession, and Eastbourne Fire Brigade would enter a display named "Fire-fighting appliances". First in the procession came the 18th-century manual engine closely followed by a horse-drawn manual engine and a selection of escape ladders. Modern engines then followed this with Chief Fire Officer Spence, Firemen Short, Ayling and Izzard. Other members of the brigade also attended. The day concluded with a firework display at the Wish Tower. The brigade had had a busy day with three call outs to chimney fires in the morning and one false alarm to Silverdale Road in the evening.

The passing of the Eastbourne Extension Act 1937 in July increased the size of the borough. The Act incorporated new areas into the borough. These embraced parts of the Parishes of Willingdon and Westham and sections of East Dean and Jevington.

False alarms are the curse of any fire brigade. Not only do they waste time and resources, but they can put lives at risk. One afternoon in early August, the brigade received a telephone call. A hairdresser's shop opposite the Archery Tavern was on fire. Sub-Officer Durrant and the fire engine proceeded to the blaze. Chief Officer Spence was to follow in his car.

On the way to the fire, at the corner of Whitley Road and Seaside, he was in collision with a cyclist. A young man, Ernest Steer received serious injuries and they rushed him to the hospital. At the Archery, the firemen discovered this had been a false alarm made by a hoaxer.

The police summoned Mr Spence in October, but after an investigation, they dismissed the charges. Although reported as travelling at 50 miles an hour with flashing light and a fire bell, the prosecutor said that he was exempt from the speed limit. This was because he was answering a fire call.

In the mid to late 1930s, they were many discussions at the Council about the building of a new fire station. They proposed it would be in Upperton Road with accommodations for the firemen. Costs of £50,000 were being mentioned, and a few councillors objected to this level of expenditure. With the coming of WW2, they put the plans on hold. The events that followed in 1943 sealed the fate of the Grove Road fire station.

****

1935 Gathering outside Grove Road Station   *Heritage Eastbourne*

Picture taken outside the Grove Road Station.

1944 NFS group.

6 WAR YEARS

As the international political situation deteriorated in the 1930s, the government commissioned the Riverdale Fire Committee on Fire Services in 1935. The committee's purpose was to look at the state of the firefighting forces throughout the country. There were 1,676 separate fire brigades spread around the country. Some of these were large and well-equipped city brigades. While others were rural and staffed by volunteers with outdated equipment. Fifty-eight of these had over twenty firemen attached to their brigades. With the passing of the 1938 Fire Brigade Act (Section 1), there were many changes. The Government made it compulsory for every local authority (County Boroughs, Urban and Rural Councils) in the country to follow new regulations. Now they had to make provision for firefighting equipment. Also, they had to maintain a firefighting service to protect life and property. Before this Act, local authorities had this power. But many didn't do this, or the service was inefficient.

Now with the anticipation of war, in 1937, after the Air Raids Precaution Act of January 1938, the Government in September created the Auxiliary Fire Service (A.F.S. unit). By late 1939, there were over 100,000 personnel made up of both men and women. They were unpaid part-time volunteers who could be called up for whole-time paid service if necessary. The Government noted the damage caused by bombing during the last war. This time they would organise the training and equipment for part-time civilian firefighters and support the regular firefighters. This recent service would provide fire engines and pumps. But the local authorities had to supply the fire stations. Every borough and urban district would have an AFS unit. They divided Eastbourne Borough into two divisions, each with a section officer in charge. These officers would arrange for each division to have ten firefighting appliances allocated to them.

To prepare for air raids and following Home Office requirements, they held an Eastbourne Round Table meeting in March 1938. At the meeting Chief Fire Officer, Mr Spence made an announcement. He stated that his service needed 300 auxiliary firemen. But up to now, only three volunteers had come forward. He said that he would continue to advertise for more volunteers for service in connection with the Air Raid Precautions.

Early on Saturday morning 16 April, the Eastbourne Fire Brigade received a call. This was for assistance to the Pevensey Brigade who were tackling a fire at the Country Club in Pevensey Bay. The building was a wooden structure and was well ablaze when the Eastbourne crews arrived. Chief Fire Officer Spence arrived with the motor pump and five men. They found the two-storey building well alight, but there was little they could do but protect surrounding houses and businesses. At eight o'clock, the Eastbourne Brigade returned to their station leaving the Pevensey crews to dampen down the Club site.

The Town Council meeting in private on Monday, 2 May 1938, accepted Chief Fire Officer Spence's 29th April letter of resignation. There were allegations made about the conduct of Mr Spence when an outside source in March brought certain facts to the notice of the Director of Public Prosecutions. This was in connection with the conduct of Mr Spence. No further details were told to the Town Council, but following police investigations, there was no case to bring criminal proceedings.

Sydney Phillips

The *Eastbourne Gazette* in the 4 May 1938 edition carried a report. It announced that the Town Council had accepted the resignation of Chief Fire Office Spence. He would leave the service at the end of the month. The Council appointed Mr S. A. Phillips as Chief Fire Officer. He joined the Eastbourne fire service in June 1932 as Second Officer and had had a distinguished career. When he was in the army, aged 18, he received the Military Medal. After that, he joined the Watford Fire Brigade in 1930 as an Engineer where he received a commendation for the rescue of three persons from a fire. He took up his new position in Eastbourne in early August.

August saw another large fire at a laundry business in Eastbourne. This was at the Fairlight Laundry in Sidley Road. Like a similar fire that occurred in 1933, the fireman succeeded in protecting the boiler room. Within an hour they had the blaze under control. They drew water from four hydrants and used over a thousand feet of hose. This was the first big fire that the newly appointed Chief Fire Officer Phillips had to deal with since his recent appointment.

There was a promise for the setting up of twenty-six new Auxiliary Fire Stations. The government agreed to equip each fire station with one fire engine or mobile trailer pump, together with crews and telephone communications.

By 25 January 1939, fourteen stations around the town were operational. The rest were awaiting equipment. They increased the Eastbourne Brigade from 13 to about 130 crew, with approximately 150 part-time members on call. The authorities expected these numbers would increase whilst hostilities continued. One of the sites they used to house fire appliances was the Corporation Bus Depot, and another was the Bacons Garage in Green Street. They also housed fire engines in the bus depot in Churchdale Road.

April 1939, and former Chief Fire Officer of Eastbourne, Mr Douglas W. Spence took up a new position in Battle. He was appointed Second Officer of the Battle Fire Brigade. In 1948 he became officer-in-charge at Uckfield and retired from service in 1955. On Monday 13 January 1958, Mr Spence aged 63, died in hospital in Hastings. His son John Spence followed in his father's footsteps and became a part-time fireman in the East Sussex Brigade.

Also, in April at the annual Brigade Dinner held in Grove Road fire station, the Deputy Mayor, Alderman J. Wheeler gave a speech. In it, he stated that the fire station "was totally inadequate for carrying out the work the brigade has to do at the present day". He said that they should extend the premises onto vacant land next to the building. The cost of this he considered would be moderate. They all agreed that they should put the idea before the council.

St. Cyprian's, a preparatory school in Summerdown Road, received substantial damage in a fire that occurred in the early hours of Sunday 14 May. Miss Beryl Nixon, a children's nurse, discovered the blaze at 5 a.m. The pupils, seventy boys and all the staff escaped safely except for one young sixteen-year-old maid. This young girl, Miss Winifred Higgs, who had only celebrated her birthday on the 12th, was attempting to leave the premises by the lifeline escape. She fell twenty feet onto a flat roof and tragically later died in hospital from her injuries. All the other staff and pupils made their escape without incidence.

Chief Officer Phillips had recently visited the school and advised them to install automatic lifelines. These were to connect the maid's rooms to an adjoining flat roof, and they installed them on the 2 May. Everyone had thought Miss Higgs had correctly fixed her lifeline. This was not the case and why she fell. The fire crews rescued four maids as they had properly secured their lifelines and travelled safely down to the adjoining flat roof. They buried Miss Higgs on Friday 19 May at Langney Cemetery.

She was a popular girl and over two hundred people attended the service including representatives from the Girl Guides, of which she was a member.

The brigade with their 100ft turntable ladder fought the fire for over two hours before getting it under control. They arrived at the fire four minutes after receiving the call at 4.59 a.m. with their motor pumps, two officers and twelve men.

EWS 875

A FIRE IN WHICH ONE LIFE WAS LOST : THE DAMAGED SECTION OF ST. CYPRIAN'S SCHOOL, EASTBOURNE, AFTER THE OUTBREAK.

On May 14 a fire broke out at St. Cyprian's School, Eastbourne. It was discovered at about 5 a.m. by a children's nurse, who gave the alarm. The seventy boys at the school were awakened and marched down the back staircases to safety. Five of the maids used an automatic fire escape and one fell from this and received fatal injuries. (A.P.)

Illustrated London News

The building was well alight when they arrived, with flames coming from the hall and the two floors above. Their first task was to rescue the young girl from the roof. Three more firemen soon joined their colleagues. Then with the turntable, they rescued the school cook from the roof.

They later reported that they had used 2,500 feet of hose to supply water from the hydrants to the pumps and ladder.

Whilst fighting the blaze, Fireman Suter had a narrow escape when the first floor gave way. He fell onto the floor below but luckily landed on his feet and escaped serious injury. At St. Mary's hospital, they reported he was suffering from shock and an injury to his left wrist.

None of the staff had received instructions on how to use the recently installed lifeline escape, although everyone had received written notices on its use. The flames destroyed the main block of the school, the roof and the dormitories. Water damage affected all the classrooms. After the fire, the school moved into temporary premises in Ascham St. Vincent's school in Carlisle Road. Then on 20 July, they removed to Whispers near Midhurst in West Sussex. Eighteen months later they moved to Rose Hill school in Alderley, Gloucestershire.

On Wednesday 14 June, Eastbourne Fire Brigade lost its former Captain and one of its best-known residents. He was an important figure in the Eastbourne Fire Brigade's history, and one of its longest-serving members. John Hounsom, who was born in the town in January 1857 died aged 83 years. As we have seen in this book, he was a well-respected man who devoted his life to the local fire service and its development. He served with the Brigade for 53 years, and for 34 years he was their Chief Officer, retiring in 1931.

20   THE EASTBOURNE GAZETTE, WEDNESDAY, JUNE 21, 1939

FORMER FIRE CHIEF'S funeral. Men of the Eastbourne Fire Brigade seen at the slow march on the way from St Anne's Church to Ocklynge Cemetery on Monday, when they formed a sorrowing escort at the funeral of a former chief, Mr J. A. Hounsom, who was fifty years a fireman.

As Captain he travelled around the country and abroad, getting details on the latest advances in training and equipment. Captain Hounsom was an honorary member of several foreign fire associations. He served as a life governor of the Widows' and Orphans' Fund and was a member of the National Fire Brigades' Association.

His funeral took place on Monday 19 June at St Anne's Church, and they buried him at Ocklynge Cemetery.

They carried his Union Jack draped coffin with his helmet, axe and belt on a fire engine. A guard of honour made up of local firemen accompanied this. Officers, firemen and retired firemen from eight county brigades also attended. Others who attended were the Mayor, Alderman A. E Rush and representatives from the council and local businesses. Over 150 people gathered to pay their respects to one of Eastbourne's finest firefighters.

The fire service was under considerable strain, and the men made frequent requests for a new fire station. As far back as December 1938, they had reported in the *Eastbourne Gazette* that the council was considering various options. They thought they would need £25,000 for the new station and could build more buildings on the site by the Art and New Technical Institute in Grove Road. Discussions continued, and in August 1939 the council was still arguing about a new fire station. One suggestion they were considering was the Bedfordwell Depot to site the building. The business Messrs Newman & Andy in September offered their premises in Grange Road to the council. But the building was not acceptable to the council, and they rejected the idea.

The present headquarters were very cramped for the firemen as they were using rooms for storage of the recently supplied air-raid precaution equipment, together with thirty delivered trailer pumps. They stated that the heating and sleeping arrangements for crews were inadequate and not fit for use. The council estimated that a new station would cost £24,000. But many councillors thought it would exceed this sum. They could recover some monies with the sale of the present site in Grove Road. Changing circumstances later scuppered these plans.

On the night of 20 March 1940, at about 22.50 hours, Heinkel He111H German bombers attacked the 5,439-ton 1921 merchant ship, *S. S. Barnhill*. (Formally known as the *Canadian Challenger*). She was sailing from Halifax, Nova Scotia to London, carrying food supplies for the war effort.

This was the first air attack by the Luftwaffe on British merchant shipping in the English Channel. At the time of the attack, she was about six miles off Langney Point, near Beachy Head, and received one bomb straight down her funnel. Another bomb hit hold No. 4, starting the fires. Four crew members lost their lives in the first assault and the ship's Captain, Michael O'Neil was thrown from the bridge onto the deck below.

A nearby Dutch merchant ship responded promptly and rescued eighteen crew of the *Barnhill*. The Eastbourne lifeboat *Jane Holland* arrived at 01.40 hours and took off a further ten survivors. But they could not find the skipper and returned to shore at 03.00 a.m.

One of the crew, the Second Engineer, died the following day in the Princess Alice Hospital. The Admiralty tug, the *Foremost 22* out of Newhaven, reported that she was at the scene, and could hear a bell ringing. It was coming from the *Barnhill*. The *Jane Holland* with a police surgeon aboard was launched again at 04.40 hours and revisited the stricken vessel.

They located Captain O'Neil and loaded him into the lifeboat and returned to shore. The ship was now drifting on the tide.

She was still ablaze when *Jane Holland* on Thursday morning returned with local firemen back to the *Barnhill*. The firemen spent many hours fighting the fire, and seven of them had a narrow escape. On the third day, the ship broke her back with two firemen on the after-deck and five colleagues below deck. They were working in the hold operating the bilge pumps. The men had to scramble to safety as the ship lurched and split in two. By dusk, they were still attacking the blaze when the Captain of the Admiralty tug ordered them off the vessel. The next morning, they returned, but the fire was stronger than the night before.

Because of the heat, the firemen had to spray water on the deck so they could safely walk. Many ruined their boots from the heat generated on the metal deck. Fireman W. A. Smith burned his feet, and they took him to hospital, where he received medical treatment for his injuries. They saved thirty-five members of the crew that morning. Captain F. M. Holden of the Newhaven tug *Foremost 22* towed the wrecked *S.S. Barnhill* to Langley Point. Today you can still see the remains of the ship's boilers near Langney Point when the tide is out.

The *Eastbourne Herald* on 16 November carried an in-depth report from Chief Fire Officer Phillips. This was a front-page story with Mr Phillips thanking all the regular firemen and AFS volunteers for their brave and efficient work. He said, "Dealing with the ravages of enemy action, the men have proved their sterling worth". The regular fire brigade has 24 firefighters, together with over 200 men and women who are members of the AFS. Besides the usual equipment, there are an additional thirty-eight trailer pumps with towing vehicles added to Eastbourne's capacity.

Another large fire occurred at Ratton Manor House, designed by F. C. Cooke and now renamed the Willingdon College. This was a college for boys, and during the war, they billeted Canadian troops in the school. This was the biggest fire that the brigade had to attend since the St. Cyprian School incidence almost two years earlier. On Tuesday morning 24 December 1940, at 2.30 a.m. the school called the fire service. And the regular firemen together with Auxiliary firemen rushed to the scene. There were over fifty men attending to the fire.

Chief Fire Officer Phillips and Second Officer Murrant arrived with three pumps and the turn-table ladder. On arrival, they found the upper stories ablaze. Fire crews concentrated their efforts on saving the west wing and ground floor.

The burning house was illuminating the sky and lighting up the entire district. By 5.30 a.m., they had the fire under control, but it was several more hours until it was extinguished. The blaze destroyed the upper floor and roof in the main building, and other rooms were badly damaged by fire and water. This is the third fire that has occurred over the years at the Manor House. It was never restored and in the 1950s they demolished the building.

On 17 January 1941, in the London Gazette, they announced Chief Fire Officer S. A. Phillips was to be awarded the M.B.E. (Civil Division). The four volunteers that were with were with him at the recent rescue were to receive the George Medal. Local newspaper the *Eastbourne Gazette* on 22 January also carried the story. This award was for a difficult rescue of people from a cellar in a bombed house in Cavendish Place in September 1940. After an air raid on the evening of 28th that demolished four shops with dwelling accommodation above, they discovered seven residents trapped in the cellars beneath. Whilst attempting the rescue, they unearthed an unexploded H.E bomb just 200 feet away. With Mr Phillips directing operations, together with four Corporation Depot volunteers, they rescued five of the seven people from the wreckage. Also commended for their bravery that day were Sub-Officer Sidney Waymark and Fireman Ernest Homewood. Later, with his wife and two daughters, Mr Phillips travelled to Buckingham Palace in London. King George VI presented him with his award.

LEAVING BUCKINGHAM PALACE 1941,
AFTER RECEIVING THE M.B.E.

D.E. Matches

Nationally the AFS was having trouble keeping up with the number of fires and damage caused by the Blitz.

The Home Secretary, Herbert Morrison announced on the 13 May 1941 that all regular brigades and the AFS would reorganise, and form the National Fire Service (N.F.S). He promised that after hostilities had ceased, the government would return control of the fire services to local councils.

So, on the 18 August 1941, the government nationalised the fire service. This was under the regulations made under the Fire Services (Emergency Provisions) Act 1941. They set up thirty-nine fire forces (Eastbourne in No.31 fire force area) in eleven designated regions and then amalgamated the AFS into the recently formed National Fire Service. Because of this Eastbourne Borough Council like councils throughout the country lost control of the management of its fire service.

The service was now under the control of the Government and the Home Office. Eastbourne Council was expected to supply fire watchers and firefighters. The government would be responsible for the cost of the fire service. But the councils would still have to pay 75% of the cost that the brigade would have cost them in peacetime. The government would take over all of the existing fire properties and equipment. The town council hoped for compensation.

This recent service used both male and female members as full and part-time crews. By August 1941, 32,200 women were serving with part-time female firefighters working every sixth night. Men were on duty every fourth night. The maximum strength of the National Fire Service, including full and part-time members, was 370,000. Of which 80,000 were women. The uniform for the NFS composed of a traditional dark blue double-breasted tunic and peaked caps.

Cooden Headquarters

The Home Office appointed Mr Phillips as NFS Divisional Chief Officer of the South Coast of England. Their headquarters (D Division, Fire Force 31) were at the requisitioned Collington Rise School in Cooden, Bexhill.

Men and women were being trained, and on a Sunday afternoon in late July, there was a presentation. The Mayor, Alderman A. E. Rush, presented badges to 70 members of the Auxiliary Fire Service (AFS) for completing their training. The AFS in Eastbourne now had 250 members which included 50 female volunteers from the Women's AFS. They needed 50 more men to bring the service up to full strength.

The war years were tough for the fire service. With Eastbourne bombed regularly, it became the most bombed town on the South coast. As a fire prevention move, emergency water supplies appeared in the town. These were static water tanks distributed throughout the town. Two of these were one in Hyde Gardens and another in Roseland's Recreation Ground. The largest tank in the town was at the junction of Langley Road and Bourne Street, which in December 1947, the council removed.

Tragedy arrived on 7 February 1943. When after days of intense bombing, four Focke Wulfe 190 aircraft launched a low-level attack at 2.57 p.m. on the town. One 500kg bomb pierced the upper floors in the fire station in Grove Road and then exploded, demolishing most of the building. The bomb detonated at ground level and took out the whole of the back of the station. Most of the two upper floors and the roof collapsed into the cellar. The front wall facing Grove Road received very little damage. There was also considerable fragmentation damage to the Free Library, New Technical Institute and nearby shops.

The bomb destroyed the fire station together with its records, and an early manual pump that had been on display. Sadly, five firemen and one firewoman, Pearl May Chitty, a National Fire Service telephonist, lost their lives that day. Three colleagues were going downstairs for a game of snooker. But one of them died in the blast. The other two firemen were lucky. One of them, Eddie Guy, was about to go off duty when his friend Duke persuaded him to stay a little longer. They were both thrown down the stairway and were buried in the rubble. Conscious, they started to shout for help, and after a while, Dr Barron and some Canadian soldiers helping in the rescue work freed them. Although the firemen were badly injured, they survived their two-hour ordeal. Fireman Duke was taken to St Mary's Hospital but later died from his injuries. His friend Fireman Guy was evacuated to a hospital out of town and made a full recovery becoming promoted to Station Officer some years later.

They held funerals for four of the firefighters at Langley Cemetery and the other two at Ocklynge Cemetery. It was some years later that the council placed a plaque commemorating the 1943 tragedy on the site of the old fire station.

By early May 1943, the fire station building had been pulled down except for the tall hose drying tower. This was still being used for practice.

This plaque commemorates the bombing of
Eastbourne Fire Station,
which previously stood on this site, and
received a direct hit at approximately 3.00 pm. on
Sunday 7th February 1943.
The following personnel were killed:-

Section Leader	J.W. BAILEY
Leading Fireman	F. MEWETT
Firewoman	P. CHITTY
Fireman	J. HUNTER
Fireman	F. DUKE
Fireman	W. GOACHER

Plaque unveiled 13 February 1997

February 1943. Front and rear of fire station.

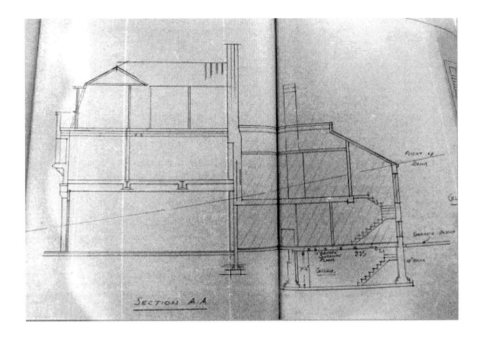

Plans from N.F.S. Fire Report   *N.A.*

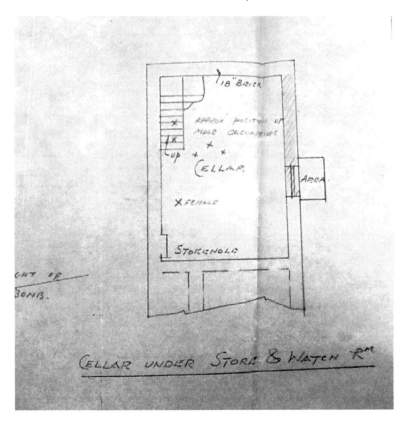

Eastbourne needed a central fire station. So, they set up a temporary one in Southfields Road. They constructed four corrugated buildings to house the fire engines. Also, the brigade used the premises in 8, Old Orchard Road (Chief Fire Officer's home) for administration.

Because of the bombing in the town, many of the red fire alarm boxes were out of action. They were either destroyed or put out of commission because of damage to the wires. Or the buildings the council had attached them to had suffered in the bombings. The service arranged for personnel of the NFS to travel around the town wiring, fitting and testing new equipment. They then connected these to the switchboard in Southfields Road which became operational in November 1944. Eighteen boxes from Meads and Green Street to Seaside were operational, plus another three in Hampden Park.

They reported in the local newspaper they had received news confirming the closure of the Willingdon Fire Station. It had closed on 31 December 1944. Anyone requiring help now had to contact the NFS in Eastbourne.

The National Fire Service began looking for a permanent solution for their headquarters. And in late 1945 they requisitioned land for the new fire station. It was May when construction began on new premises in Bourne Street. Because of the urgent need for a new headquarters, members of the fire service built the Bourne Street fire station. They equipped it with a dormitory, and bath and shower rooms. There was a sizeable mess room with a full-size billiards table, dart-board, radio and comfortable chairs for the crews to relax in between 'shouts'. There were offices, workshops, hose repair and store shop, together with a new switchboard. A 60ft drill and hose drying tower was built.

On 18 March 1946, the National Fire Service moved its operations from Southfields Road to Bourne Street their new headquarters. In the new Watch Room, there is a large signal board for receiving calls.

Dave Freeman

Watch room at Bourne Street

When someone telephones reporting a fire, the signal board automatically registers the street and prints the date and details on a ticker-tape. Should they receive a call from one of the twenty-five street alarms, they record this with a special code onto tape. Bells ring in the fire station, and within seconds they dispatch a fire engine. Every time a man goes on duty in the Watch Room, he tests every line by pressing a set of buttons. The buttons are set out in pairs, checking the line. Should there be a fault, it will automatically show up on a dial on the panel.

In the *Eastbourne Gazette* on the 1 May, Divisional Officer Phillips gave an interview. This was about the many false fire alarms that the brigade was receiving. In one week, they received three such calls. He stated that if they caught a person making these calls, then there were heavy penalties. The penalty for the hoaxer could be a £100 fine or imprisonment for three months. As many of the hoax calls received were from children, Divisional Officer Phillips and Chief Officer Short said that teachers at schools should educate the children about the dangers of making false calls. If anyone wanted to see the fire engines and learn about the fire service, then they would be happy to show them around the fire station. Their last words were a warning that they had set up traps and would catch hoaxers.

National Fire Service

Opening of New Fire Station

BY

His Worship the Mayor of Eastbourne,
Alderman C. Martin, J.P.

BOURNE STREET, EASTBOURNE
Friday, 10th, May, 1946
at 3.0 p.m.

Dave Freeman

Official Program

The Mayor, Alderman E. C. Martin, J.P., officially opened the new fire station on Friday the 10 May 1946 by ringing the fire bell. Accompanying him was Mr A. S. Hutchinson, C.V.O., Principal Assistant to the Secretary of State, Mr A. P. L. Sullivan C.B.E., M.M., Mr A. A. Davis O.B.E. and Mr C. Birch O.B.E. from the fire services. Divisional Officer Phillips greeted them, and the Mayoress unveiled a memorial tablet to the firefighters who died in 1943 when bombs fell on Grove Road fire station. After a tour of the station, they served tea to the guests.

Early in August a party of twenty senior fire officers, who were attending the National Fire Service training college at Saltdean, visited Eastbourne. The Eastbourne service sent an invitation to the officers and invited them to inspect the new fire station in Bourne Street. All the group was impressed with the drill tower and method used to dry hoses. And some said they would adopt a similar system in their areas when they returned.

The Watch Committee in November 1947 received a report from Chief Fire Officer (designate) Phillips. This was regarding the reconstitution of the Eastbourne Fire Brigade. In it, he recommended that the brigade should consist of, a whole-time senior staff of Chief Fire Officer, a Deputy Chief Fire Officer, two Company Officers and four Leading firemen. Also required were thirty firemen, a clerk and watch room attendant and from the retained list, two Leading firemen and ten firemen. The council noted that this was more than the 1938 establishment, but less than the present allowed NFS force. A provisional cost given by the Borough Treasurer, less Government grant, would be £17,162 per year. This was considerably more than the 1938-39 cost of £5,377. East Sussex County Council had requested that Eastbourne Borough fire service should cover the Parishes of Friston, East Dean, Jevington and Willingdon. When asked, Chief Fire Officer Phillips stated it was possible. But pointed out that Eastbourne covered two retained fire stations. One was in Polegate and the other one in Pevensey. He suggested that the County Council should take responsibility for the Parishes of Polegate, Westham and Pevensey.

In January 1948, the Borough Council received a letter from the Home Office (Fire Service Department). This was on their plans for the future of the fire service. Chief Fire Officer Phillips said that his earlier recommendations in November 1947 were correct, but agreed that they could increase the number of retained firemen from twelve to thirteen men. The Committee said they would forward his comments to the Home Office.

Divisional Officer S. A. Phillips spoke to an *Eastbourne Gazette* reporter in early February about the varied work of his men. During the last year, the brigade received calls to help rescue birds from chimneys, dogs in drains, cats from trees and men locked out of their house. There were thirty-eight incidents during the year, and this was beside their normal duties to fight fires and assist the police. The brigade responded to 271 call outs of which 32 were outside the county borough. They reported the only fatal casualty during the year was a dog, and the financial loss caused by fires during 1947 was the lowest for a very long time. He then listed some properties that the brigade had received calls from. They were the Saffrons Pavilion and Albion Hotel. Also fires in Pevensey Bay and Susans Road, North and Meads Street, Seaside, Royal Sussex Crescent and a gorse fire at St Anthony's Avenue.

He stressed the importance of the public to use fire alarm boxes situated around the town. Or use a public telephone box where calls are free by pressing the emergency button.

In March, the Town Council announced an increase of 10d in the £ to the rates. One reason given for this increase was the cost of the return of the Fire Brigade to Council control. They estimated this would be an additional £13,211 for the current year.

The town hosted a conference of the Institution of Fire Engineers in June. Over 100 local authorities were represented together with 30 Ministries and Government departments.

Tuesday, 12 October, just after 6.30 in the evening, a passing taxi driver heard an explosion coming from The Technical Institute in Grove Road. He contacted the fire brigade, who were on scene within minutes with four engines. The first and second floor was well alight when the brigade arrived, but they had the blaze under control in three-quarters of an hour. It took another half hour to extinguish the fire completely. Fire crews used four lines of hose and the turn-table ladder to subdue the flames. The Council had stored paints, oils and timber in the building.

Early December and the fire service held their annual dance and fundraiser at the Winter Garden. This was the second such dance held since the end of the war and over six hundred people attended.

****

Dave Freeman

1943 N.F.S. Outside Grove Road FS.

7 RETURNED FIRE APPLIANCES.

As promised by the government, they handed back control of the local fire services to Councils and Boroughs. The appliances returned to Eastbourne were.......

1924 Dennis Pump Escape with 50ft Wheeled Escape.
1932 Morris Escape tender with 50ft Wheeled Escape.
1932 Merryweather Turntable Ladders.
1935 Dennis Limousine Pump with 35ft Ajax Extending Ladders.

"Fire" February 1936.

Eastbourne Fire Brigade took over other appliances that the NFS had gained whilst they were in charge. The NFS. had modified some of these vehicles and they were soon replaced.

1940/1 Dennis trailer Pumps 350/500 g.p.m (2).
1941 Austin Towing vehicles (20).
1941/3 Beresford Stork trailer pumps 120 g.p.m (2).
1943 Dodge Water tender with 450 gal. water tank.
1943 Austin Salvage tender.

****

Michael Garrett

Bourne Street.

Chief Fire Officer Short. 1956-1964

8 EASTBOURNE BOROUGH FIRE BRIGADE

As promised and following the Fire Service Act 1947, the government handed back control of the fire services to local authorities on 1 April 1948. Most services now came under the East Sussex Fire Brigade, which covered an area of 781 sq. miles with 28 fire stations. Borough towns such as Brighton, Eastbourne and Hastings had their fire services. The new Eastbourne County Borough Fire Brigade with one fire station covered Eastbourne. This was an area of 10 sq. miles. They came under the local authority of the Watch Committee.

There was an inspiring advert placed in the *Eastbourne Gazette* on 21 April 1948 by Chief Fire Officer S. A. Phillips. He was inviting applications for retained firemen from men aged 21 to 40 years. They would work from the recently opened Bourne Street Fire Station. On offer was £15 per annum retaining fee plus a fee for fires attended. He stated "here is an opportunity to perform a useful and interesting service which can be made into a remunerative hobby".

It is early evening on the 31 July when the fire station receives a call. It's from the Town Hall, and engines rushed to the scene. When they arrive, no fire is found. On further inspection, they discovered that the sun had set off the automatic alarms. It was beating down at 90 degrees on the sensors. Never mind a good practice for the crews and so time to reposition the sensors.

The Fire Service National Benevolent Fund had asked all brigades to take parties of orphan children from firefighter's families for the summer holidays. These were children aged between six and fourteen years. Eastbourne had been the first brigade to answer their appeal.

They funded the cost of the holiday from generous donations which came from the Mayor, friends of Chief Fire Officer Phillips and the Eastbourne Fire Service Social Club. In early August they arranged the first trip.

Fifteen orphans of firefighters from other areas in the country whose families had suffered fire service deaths in the war were treated to a week's holiday in Eastbourne. Leading Fireman Payne and his wife travelled up to London Victoria by train to meet the group. They escorted them back to Eastbourne.

On arrival at Eastbourne at 3.40 p.m., the Mayor greeted them and took them to the fire station for tea. They would accommodate all children for the week in the homes of members of the brigade. The Social Club organised entertainment and trips for the children during their stay in Eastbourne.

At the annual general meeting of the National Fire Brigades Association held in Chichester in December, they elected Chief Fire Officer S. A. Phillips as their president. He had only just returned to Eastbourne in April after serving during the war as Divisional Officer for half of Sussex and part of Kent.

In 1948, after the Civil Defence Act, the AFS was re-established and worked with the newly formed Civil Defence Corps. The Government was concerned over the deteriorating relations with the Soviet Union and war in Europe seemed a possibility. The Government disbanded the AFS and Civil Defence on the 31st of March 1968.

Chief Fire Officer Phillips's report for the year 1948 stated that the brigade had received 301 call outs. All but 16 were from within the borough. Most of the calls they received were for minor events that involved children playing with matches, together with chimney fires, or articles of clothing left too close to the fire. Flooding, the rescue of cats and helping residents who had locked themselves out of their premises had caused many call outs. He stated that the brigade had rescued six people from fires with the aid of the escape ladders. Fire prevention and advice was now a recent service offered by the brigade. This was the Fire Protection Scheme introduced in April 1948, and by early January 1949, they had inspected no fewer than 409 premises and given advice.

These included such places as hotels, schools, hospitals, business premises and places of public entertainment. Mr Phillips also reported that there were now 1,700 hydrants in the borough. The brigade under the command of Chief Fire Officer Phillips and his Deputy, Mr Murrant now comprises of whole-time ranks of 2 Station Officers, 5 Leading Firemen and 31 firemen. Two Leading Firemen and thirteen Firemen make up the retained section. Their current equipment includes 2 pump escapes, 4 pumping appliances, a turntable ladder and salvage tender. The escapes and pumping appliances each carry two sets of self-contained breathing apparatus.

Leading Fireman Payne and Fireman Gray escaped serious injury in early February 1949. They were attending an incident at the George House in Westham when a gas meter exploded. The fire in a cupboard under the stairs contained a gas meter, and the blaze ignited the gas. The blast threw both firemen through a window and into the street, but they escaped injury.

In June, they list Polegate Fire Station for closure. After a public inquiry, held by the Hailsham Rural District Council with Lt-Colonel Sir Vivian Henderson presiding, they agreed to close the fire station. They described it as "a wartime hut in a bad state of repair". The Home Office accepted the council's recommendations for the closure. It noted that there had not been a Volunteer Fire Service in the town before 1938-1939. Chief Fire Officer of the East Sussex Fire Brigade, Mr Mees, had supported the closure of the fire station. He said the Hailsham, Eastbourne, Pevensey and Seaford Brigades could adequately cover the area.

Eastbourne won two events out of four at the annual trials organised by the National Fire Brigades' Association, South Coast District. They held these at Oaklands Park in Chichester where the brigade received a cup. The *Eastbourne Herald* carried a photo of the team in their 20th August edition.

On Tuesday 27 September, Eastbourne hosted a visit from the French town of Evreux. Eastbourne Council had invited them to play a football match and watch a fire-fighting display by the brigade. The match between the Evreux football team and Eastbourne Town would take place on Wednesday afternoon. The French team were a champion team from Normandy and recently promoted to the French Amateur League. When the visitors arrived, they took them to the Winter Garden to watch a display of old-thyme dancing.

The following morning, they escorted the party to the fire station in Bourne Road where Ald. E. C. Martin with Chief and Deputy Fire Officers Phillips and Murrant greeted them. The Corporation Catering Department provided refreshments for the visitors.

There was one hour of entertainment with the brigade showing off their prowess in rescuing someone from a burning building. They followed this with an excellent display using their turntable ladder and lowering a fireman by rope-sling to the ground. Then they asked a guest to sound the fire alarm. Crews showed how speedily they could muster and be ready to attend a fire.

Chief Officer Phillips gave a brief speech and mentioned this was the third time the brigade had given a display to French visitors to the town. The town had previously entertained the France-British Society, a football team from Paris, and had now welcomed the Evreux football team.

Many people attended, and they held the football match at the Saffrons. The home team won by 9 - 2. Afterwards, there was a civic reception and dinner at the Cavendish Hotel. This is the third time the two football clubs had played each other. Evreux AC last visited Eastbourne in September 1948 and the Eastbourne football team promised to visit Evreux the following year and looked forward to a return match with them.

Eastbourne Town FC players with Deputy Mayor, Alderman E. C. Martin and officials with seventy-five supporters travelled to France in May 1949.

The cost to the Eastbourne supporters who travelled was 4,500 francs each and covered all costs from arrival at Dieppe on Saturday until the return there the following evening. The exchange rate was 1,060 francs to the pound. Cambolle Stadium hosted the match on a sunny Sunday afternoon when Eastbourne FC defeated the French team 1 – 3. Nearly two thousand spectators attended the match. By coincidence in Paris, there was a football match between England and France. Again, England won, and the score was the same as in Evreux. England 3, France 1. The local teams met again in June 1950 at the Cambolle Stadium, and Eastbourne won that match, three goals to two.

The Chief Fire Officer wanted to keep his brigade up to the highest state of efficiency. At the Watch Committee meeting in January 1950, he made a few recommendations. These were for the conversion of a water tender, at an estimated cost of £600 and a towing tender at an estimated cost of £300. He also proposed installing a two-way radio system on two of the brigade's fire appliances, and their staff car. There were some councillors against this idea, but they agreed with the principle and would forward his suggestions to the Finance Committee.

At the end of March, His Majesty's Inspector Mr F. Dann. O.B.E., visited Eastbourne. He was coming to inspect the brigade and award various medals to the firemen. The inspection was made at Bourne Street with thirty-seven firemen present. After the parade, Mr Dann presented long service medals to six members of the brigade. Also, safety driving certificates issued by the Royal Society of Prevention of Accidents were presented by Alderman Richards to nineteen firemen.

The *Eastbourne Herald* in April carried a report that the Home Office had permitted the Fire Brigade to use the Police wireless system. The Chief Fire Officer had recommended the idea to the Watch Committee. And they approved the idea subject to tests being carried out.

July saw the annual tournament organised by the British Fire Services Association which they held at Elm Grove playing fields in Hampden Park. Thirty-eight teams from around the country took part and camped in tents on the grounds. Eastbourne was the only public fire service team to compete, as the others involved in the competition were either works or factory teams. There were brigades from Dunlop, Bournville, Daimler, Standard, and Morris Cowley factory teams. Over 400 men attended the event and there was no charge to the public to come and watch. The Eastbourne Brigade won the Marlborough Cup for the escape drill and on Tuesday evening, the corporation arranged a dinner and concert. They held this in the officers' mess at the camp at Elm Grove. The Winter Garden Orchestra and Gordon Rider provided the entertainment. Also, the baritone, Eastbourne Fireman Kirkland entertained the meeting. There were speeches and thanks given to the Mayor for his hospitality. It had been thirty years since the Association last held their gathering and camped in Eastbourne. They looked forward to returning in the future.

There was damage to two houses in a fire on Monday morning 17 July. At nine o'clock, Mrs P. L. Thomson, a student at the Eastbourne School of Art, who lived in the property, discovered the fire. She rang the fire station immediately. Within two minutes, the brigade arrived, and firefighters wearing breathing apparatus entered the four-storied house in Upperton Gardens. The brigade used their 100ft turntable ladder as a water tower from which they directed hoses down onto the blazing roof. The fire had originated in an attic at No.9 and spread to the neighbouring property at No.7. Before the firemen could bring the fire under control, the roof of both buildings collapsed. Strong winds fanned the blaze, and it was one hour and forty-five minutes before the firemen extinguished the fire.

Also in July, Chief Fire Officer S. A. Phillips presented his report for the previous year. In it, he stated that there were thirty-nine fires in the borough. Careless disposal of lighted matches and hot ashes caused these. Children playing with matches began sixteen fires. The brigade received 355 calls, of which 27 were false alarms. Call outs varied between fires in commercial and residential buildings and calls to broken-down cars and grass/forest fires. There were thirty-two call outs to areas outside of the borough.

There was also a report in the 26 July issue of the *Eastbourne Gazette* about improvements to the fire engines. The council decided they would replace the 1924 Dennis pump escape with a new appliance. They would overhaul the Dodge water tender and install a new power-driven pump and hose reel equipment to the Austin tender.

August and the *Eastbourne Herald* on the 19th reported that members of the Rotary Club visited the fire station. The firemen entertained the Rotarians and their wives with displays of hook ladder drills and a tour of the fire station and watch room.

Following the success of the reintroduction of the flower shows in Eastbourne, the Fire Brigade Social Club decided they would hold their annual show. Station Officer P. Short had suggested the idea. The social club agreed. The first of these took place on Saturday 2nd September at the fire station in Bourne Street. There were over two hundred entries, and the Mayor presented the prizes. They donated all the proceeds from the sale of fruits and vegetables to the National Benevolent Fund.

In the evening, Mayor, Alderman R. Croft presented Leading Fireman A. Green with a diploma. This was for completing his course at the Institute of Fire Engineers.

E/B Gazette 6 September 1950

Over 700 people including the Mayor and Mayoress, Alderman and Mrs R. J. S. Scott, attended the annual fireman's ball held in the Winter Garden on Wednesday evening 11 October. The firemen set up a direct telephone line from the brigade headquarters to the Winter Garden in case they received an alarm. Also, they stationed three fire appliances outside the venue. Some of the firemen attended the ball in uniform ready to respond if needed although there were crews on duty stationed at the headquarters in Grove Road. Music was provided by Gordon Rider and his orchestra playing modern dance and old-time. The dance sub-committee of the Fire Brigade Social Club organised the ball in aid of fire service charities.

The Eastbourne Brigade's water tender was called to assist the Hailsham and Herstmonceux fire services early in the morning on Saturday 18 November. There was a fire in a bungalow at Mill Lane, Hellingly and it was not until half-past three that they brought the fire under control. The occupant, 70-year-old Walter Mann, perished in the fire and his bungalow was destroyed. They held the inquest at Hellingly Hospital on 21 November and informed that Mr Mann was a solicitor's clerk and a former director of Radio Luxembourg.

In the New Year honours list, they awarded Chief Fire Officer Phillips the King's Police and Fire Service medal. The Duke of Norfolk, as Lord Lieutenant of Sussex, came to Eastbourne to present him with his medal.

They held the ceremony in the Council Chamber on Monday 9 April 1951 where twenty members of the brigade formed a guard of honour in the Town Hall lobby. Mr Phillips had joined the fire service in 1930 and was appointed Chief Fire Officer in Eastbourne in 1938.

"More Auxiliary Firemen Still Wanted" was a headline in *Eastbourne Herald* on the 12 May 1951. The Chief Fire Officer had sent out an appeal to ex-members of the National Fire Service, asking them to support the Auxiliary Fire Service in Eastbourne. They needed 110 auxiliaries. But in March there were only twenty men and seven women in the auxiliary service.

He reminded everyone that men over thirty and women over eighteen years were eligible to join. The training was four to five hours a month and the regular fire service needed their support.

Eastbourne Borough bought a new Dennis fire engine with a 50ft escape ladder in June/July. This had an enclosed cabin and could pump 1,000 gallons per minute. This new engine also had a V.H.F radio, a searchlight and two bells. The duty officer could operate one of these electrically.

When the need arose, brigades helped each other out. There was an enormous fire in Seaford on Wednesday evening, the 8th of August. The Champion Electrical Manufacturing Works in Steyne Road was blazing fiercely, so the East Sussex Fire Brigade asked for assistance from Eastbourne. The factory manufactured television and radio sets and employed about 250 people. Bourne Street received the call at 10.30 p.m. Two motor pumps and an Eastbourne crew of eight firefighters set off for Seaford.

There they joined the Seaford, Newhaven and Lewes sections of the East Sussex Brigades. Deputy Chief Officer W. Holland was in overall charge. There was danger of the fire spreading to adjoining buildings and petrol stores as there was a garage just a few yards away from the factory. But favourable winds blew the fire away from these structures. Whilst they were fighting the fire, part of the roof of the building collapsed. This caused a wall to fall towards three of the Eastbourne crew. But with quick action, they escaped injury. Large groups of people came out to watch the proceedings. The Eastbourne crews were withdrawn and arrived back in Eastbourne at 3.15 a.m. on Thursday. The fire was still smouldering at 6.30 a.m. on Thursday and the blaze destroyed the factory which was never rebuilt.

Friday 17 August and late in the afternoon the brigade got a call to a fierce fire in Cavendish Place. They dispatched three fire appliances to tackle the blaze in one of the shops. A few days later, early on Sunday evening the 19th, the brigade received a call to a farm fire in East Dean. They sent a water tender to the blaze and got assistance from the Seaford Fire Brigade. A large 50-ton haystack was on fire.

The Eastbourne firemen stayed on scene for forty hours and prevented the fire spreading to crops in adjoining fields.

*E/*B Gazette 22 August 1951

Fire crews at Cavendish Place fire.

The National Joint Council recently met (1951) and reviewed the grading and salary of the firefighting services. They had now placed Eastbourne on the lowest category, which meant that it would put the Chief Officer on a lower scale and have his salary reduced by £125 per year. The Council currently base the old system on rateable values. Under the new system, they would base it on population, fire risk and establishments. The National Council wanted to reduce the number of fire authority grades from ten to seven.

The Watch Committee held a meeting when Mr Phillips, the Chief Fire Officer, submitted a report. He asked if they had advised the National Joint Council of the significant increase of population in the town during the summer when the number of residents of the town could double. He advised the Committee that with the agreement with the County Council, they had increased fire cover for an extra acreage of some 12,000, with a population of 10,000. Mr Phillips urged the Committee to contact the Home Office and ask that they increase Eastbourne's grading

The Committee agreed to his request. Mr Phillips also mentioned that the cost of maintenance for the Bourne Street fire station would continue to rise as the buildings were mainly of a pre-fabricated type of construction.

Storms and torrential rain hit Eastbourne in September as reported in the *Eastbourne Chronicle* on 15th. There was substantial flooding in the town and also in Willingdon and Polegate.

It was a Wednesday morning when the storm suddenly struck and lasted over three-quarters of an hour. Eastbourne Fire Brigade received over eighteen calls for help. This was the most calls they had received in one day for over fifteen years. The fire service reported that it was the busiest day they'd had since Friday, July 10, 1936, when they answered 120 rescue calls.

October 17 saw the Fire Brigade Social Club's annual dance held at the Winter Garden with over six hundred people attending. The dancing and merriment carried on until 1 a.m. Chief Fire Officers from Hastings and East Sussex fire brigades attended with their wives. In case of a call out, Eastbourne fire service positioned their escapes and appliances outside of the Winter Garden in readiness for a quick departure.

There were a busy few days in late October when the brigade received four call outs in two days. On Tuesday afternoon they received a call from the Oban Hotel. They received another call that evening to a house fire in Penhale Road. Early Wednesday morning the Eastbourne Tyre Co in Fort Road reported a fire in their showroom. Also, that morning the brigade attended with the Hailsham and Pevensey Bay appliances at a fire. This was at Priesthawes farm in Hankham. They extinguished all the fires quickly without injury to any persons.

In November Mr F. Dann, one of the H.M. Inspectors of Fire Service visited the town. Whilst here, he and the Mayor, Alderman R. J. S. Croft presented Royal Life Saving Society's bronze medallions to Firemen K. Burns and R. Simmonds.

Also, in November, after a meeting in the Bourne Street fire station. The firemen agreed not to support a call from the Fire Brigades Union for a forty-eight-hour strike. The dispute was over pay and equal wages with the police. Local authorities had offered them 15s., but the Union wanted a 35s weekly increase. The local branch stated they would consider further calls for action on behalf of their members. In January, the Chief Fire Officer wrote to the Watch Committee about the question of pay for the firemen. The Committee refused to comment stating the matter was now at arbitration.

The wholesale greengrocery firm of Messrs F. G. Pinker Ltd suffered a big fire at their warehouse. This was in South Street when fire consumed the building.

On Tuesday evening, the 11th December, someone telephoned the police to inform them of the fire, and they contacted the fire brigade. The brigade quickly dispatched three fire appliances and the turntable ladder to the scene. Under the charge of Chief Fire Office S. A. Phillips, the blaze was under control within thirty-two minutes. It had destroyed the building with just charred beams and the outer walls remaining.

The firemen removed lorries from the yard, but the fire destroyed the grocery stock. Surrounding buildings did not suffer any damage because of the prompt action of the fire crews.

There was a report in the *Herald Chronicle* on 5 January 1952 that nineteen members of the Eastbourne Fire Brigade would soon receive diplomas. These were from the Royal Society for the Prevention of Accidents.

On 21 December 1951 there was a terrible fire that destroyed a warehouse at Broad Street goods station, in London. One of the local brigades to respond to the fire was Whitefriars station. Eight men went to fight the blaze, but only one returned. Two firemen died, and five were taken to hospital badly burnt. One of the men taken to hospital had his leg amputated due to his injuries. On 28 January 1952, they held a service in St Pauls Cathedral, London, where over 2,000 people attended. Brigades from around the country were present. Eastbourne's Deputy Chief Office J. Murrant, Fireman F. Kirkland and Fireman E. Jay travelled to London to attend the memorial service.

There was a national campaign to recruit new volunteers for the AFS in April. Posters were displayed around the town and at Bourne Street fire station there was a week of displays of rescue work. This included a fireman hanging from a line and being lowered from the turntable ladder.

Demonstrations carried on every day of the week. They invited residents in the evening to watch two fire service action films, "The Waking Point" and "Fire's the Enemy" to be shown at 7.15 p.m. at the fire station. Spectators were told that "auxiliary firemen get almost the same training as regulars". Chief Fire Officer Phillips told the *Eastbourne Chronicle* "that the present strength was 36 men and women, compared with a permitted strength of 110".

In August, the Mayor, Alderman E. C. Martin presented twenty certificates to firemen. They held the presentation in the recreation room at Bourne Street fire station. The awards were for safe driving in the two years of 1950-1951. The Royal Society for the Prevention of Accidents issued them. The Mayor also presented a diploma to Fireman H. M. Hendry. He passed his graduate examination at the Institution of Fire Engineers. At the presentation, Chief Fire Officer Phillips reminded the men that they must always obey the traffic rules when attending a fire.

He said all the drivers are hand-picked and well trained. He advised the men that "we are a little different from normal road users" but "we are not allowed by law to disregard driving regulations".

THE ALL-NIGHT FIRE TEAM checks equipment ready for any emergency.

AUX. FIREMAN J. CHERRYMAN was in H.M. Armed Forces during the war and is now employed by a well known Motor Engineering Firm in Eastbourne.

He finds time to enjoy training as a fireman to **"BE PREPARED"** in case of emergency.

WHY NOT JOIN HIM?

A few hours a month is all we ask.

HELP US TO FIGHT THE NATION'S DEADLY ENEMY "FIRE."

BE READY
"If the Bells Go Down"

JOIN YOUR LOCAL **A.F.S.**

Details at the FIRE STATION, BOURNE STREET

Following on from the April campaign the Eastbourne *Herald Chronicle* carried an advert on the 17 October asking men to join the Eastbourne AFS.

In the yearly report by Chief Fire Officer Phillips, he said that there were 356 calls to the brigade in the year ending March 31st 1952, with no serious fires reported. This was thirty-six more call outs than in the previous year, and the highest number since the brigade returned to control by the borough. His report then said that twenty calls came from outside of the borough. The brigade recorded no fatalities, but there were twenty-one false alarms recorded with six malicious calls received.

He also reported that the "completion of the new building on the vacant site in Ashford Road has considerably eased the problem of the accommodation of appliances". This has added to the efficiency of the Bourne Street fire station. Also, in the report, he said that there were 1,802 hydrants in the area, which the brigade regularly inspects and test. Six members of the brigade have qualified for the silver medal of the British Fire Services Association for long service and good conduct. He mentioned that members of the public, and some organisations, had visited the fire station and enjoyed the drills and demonstrations that his men presented. This was an excellent opportunity for the brigade to advise about fire prevention and precautions.

A new group was being formed – the Junior Fire Officers Association, which caters for ranks of sub-officer and leading firemen. With the support of the Chief Fire Officer Phillips, they wanted the council to recognise this new union.

He reported that six members of the Eastbourne Fire Brigade were eligible to join the association. The council could not agree and decided to wait until there was national approval of the new group.

Sadly, Eastbourne's Chief Fire Officer Sydney A. Phillips, aged 55, died on the 30 June 1953. He had been ill and off work since the previous November. He had joined Eastbourne in June 1932 as second officer and became Chief Fire Officer after Mr Short resigned in 1938.

As already noted, when the government nationalised the fire service in 1941, they appointed him Divisional Chief Officer. He had 60 brigades and 3,000 personnel under his command. After the denationalisation in 1947, he returned to his old position of Chief Officer at Eastbourne. Mr Phillips was one of Eastbourne's officials to receive the Queen's Coronation Medal in June.

In November 1952 he had to go into hospital in Brighton but returned home a month later.

They covered his coffin with the Union Jack and placed it on a large Pump Escape, which they carried from his home to the church. Besides the regular firemen, auxiliary firemen and civil defence personnel attending there were colleagues from brigades throughout the country. They formed a guard of honour at the entrance to the church and carried the coffin inside for the service. This was one of the largest turnouts of civic representatives and officials that Eastbourne had seen for many years. After the service, they took the coffin to Brighton Crematorium. Mr Phillips left a widow and two married daughters.

THE BODY of Chief Fire Officer S. A. Phillips is lifted by his comrades from the fire engine that bore it to Upperton Congregational Church, where the funeral service took place on Wednesday.

E/B Herald Chronicle 11 July 1953

At the Town Council meeting in July, the councillors held a silent tribute in memory of Chief Fire Officer Phillips. Then the Mayor, Alderman E. C. Martin said in praise "he was a very fine man and loyal officer of the brigade and will be sadly missed". They agreed to send a letter of sympathy to his wife. In August the Corporation agreed to pay Mrs S. A. Phillips a weekly gratuity, this was in addition to the widows benefit under the Firemen's Pension Scheme of £66 13s 4d a year.

The Watch Committee advertised the position of Chief Fire Officer at a salary of £750 a year, rising to £875 and the standing sub-committee would select applications.

Summer had arrived, and the fire brigade held its fourth annual flower show in September 1953. This was at the Bourne Street fire station, and Eastbourne's Deputy Mayor gave out the prizes. After the show, they held an auction and sold the exhibits. They donated the proceeds to the Fire Service Benevolent Fund.

David Holt

AFS 1950's

Outside Bacons Garage, Green Street   *Patrick Smith.*

Patrick Smith

Outside Bourne Street fire station

Patrick Smith

AFS Crew in Maidstone

Coverplas Ltd. 20 May 1972   ESRO

Firemen at work

Dave Freeman

100-FEET LADDER IN ACTION

PERCHED ON THE TOP of the escape, a fireman fights the flames. Another picture on page 11.

Eastbourne Gazette 19 July 1950

Marine Laundry Fire June 1933. *ESRO*

Pier Fire 1970

E/B Herald Chronicle 5 September 1953

On the 3rd of September, Eastbourne-born Charles Murrant took up the vacant position of Chief Fire Officer. Mr Murrant had been the Deputy Fire Officer under Mr Phillips. He had served in the Eastbourne Brigade since 1926- first as a part-time fireman and in 1931 as a full-time member. During the war, he was a Divisional Officer in the NFS based in Tunbridge Wells. When the government returned control of the fire brigades to the local authorities in 1948, he became Deputy Chief Officer in Eastbourne. His father also served as an engineer in the service for thirty-five years. Seven candidates had applied for the position.

The following month Mr F. Dann, an inspector of fire brigades, visited Eastbourne where the local firemen put on a large display and practice in the Bourne Street rear yard. First, the men were drawn into ranks and then inspected by Mr Dann, Alderman R. J. Croft, the Deputy Mayor, and the Deputy and Chief Fire Officers. They presented four firemen with Long Service Medals. The men on parade, many of whom were off duty, started drills and rescues. They used their pump and turntable ladder.

When they had finished, Mr Dann congratulated the brigade on its drills and the high standard of discipline on parade. He also told them that the Firemen's Union would soon introduce a new twenty years' service medal.

A dispute in late November between the Fire Brigade Union and East Sussex Fire Brigade resulted in five of their fire stations deciding to stop working voluntary overtime. As reported in the *Eastbourne Gazette* firemen at Crowborough, East Grinstead, Lewes, Newhaven and Uckfield would revert to the standard 60-hour week. Discussions were being held between the East Sussex Brigade and the National Joint Council for Local Authorities Fire Brigades. Chief Fire Officer Murrant stated Eastbourne was not involved with these discussions as Eastbourne had a different duty system.

In the *Herald Chronicle* on 28 November the council invited tenders from interested companies for the supply of a new appliance for the brigade. This was for a Water Tender (Type B) they wished to add to the fleet in the year starting 1st April 1954.

In the same newspaper, the Watch Committee announced that Station Officer P. Short would be appointed Deputy Chief Fire Officer. They would grant a £50 a year increase in salary for his new position.

Reports in the *Herald Chronicle* 27 February 1954 confirmed that the Watch Committee had agreed to buy a new water tender for the fire brigade. They awarded the contract to Messrs Mansfields Ltd of Cornfield Road, as they were the lowest of twelve tenders that the Committee had received. The cost of the new appliance, a Bedford, was £2,418. In October the brigade bought 600ft of a two-and-a-half-inch rubber-lined hose. The cost per foot was 3s 5d, not the cheapest price quoted but a far superior quality, the Chief Fire Officer said.

In March, Chief Fire Officer Murrant and Fire Prevention Officer Mr P. C. Short gave the *Herald Chronicle* a lengthy interview about the dangers of fire. Mr Short had recently returned from a four-month extensive course on fire prevention at the Fire Service College in Dorking, Surrey.

They reminded everyone of the dangers of inflammable fluids and leaving children unattended. Also, the risk of cigarettes being left around the home. Chimney fires had recently been an enormous concern for the brigade, together with what they called "amateur electrics". They requested that should one discover a fire, the first thing to do was contact the fire brigade and not to extinguish the fire oneself. The newspaper covered the interview in a full-page article on 22 May.

The Watch Committee announced a few days later an increase in pay of 7s 6d a week for sub-officers and firemen. They would also make adjustments for officers and female ranks. The annual net cost of the increase would be £600.

A few weeks later, the *Eastbourne Gazette* carried an article about the "singing fireman". Sub-Officer Frank Kirkland, who had been in the fire service since 1942, used to entertain his colleagues at the various functions that they attended. The son of a recognised baritone opera singer, Frank had taken lessons for his singing. But did not want to make it his profession. He said that he enjoyed being a fireman and serving the community.

On 7 July, the Borough wishing to sell their 1932 Morris Escape placed an advert in the *Eastbourne Gazette*.

COUNTY BOROUGH of Eastbourne Fire Brigade. Offers are invited for the purchase of a 1932 27 h.p. Morris Commercial Escape Carrier fitted with hose reel equipment and carrying a 50ft. Bayley wooden wheeled escape.—Offers should be sent to the Chief Fire Officer. Fire Station, Bourne-street, Eastbourne. not later than August 30. 1954.

WHEN A SWARM OF BEES came to rest in a tree in Seaside one afternoon last week it took the combined efforts of the Fire Brigade and an apiarist to catch them. This picture was taken by a reader, Mr M. Ryder, of 68 Ash-road, Leeds, who was on holiday in Eastbourne.

E/B Gazette 7 July 1954

Some jobs that the firemen are called to need help from other experts. A swarm of bees being removed from a tree in Seaside.

On the 28 August, the *Eastbourne Herald* interviewed Chief Fire Officer Murrant. They asked him about the operation of the twenty-eight street fire alarms situated around the town. G.P.O. under-ground cables connect some of these directly to the fire station, but most relied on overhead wires, which the firemen check and maintained. They tested the alarms weekly and the wiring three times a day.

Each alarm box has an individual number, so when the brigade received a call, a tape machine stamped the date, time and alarm box code number. They kept this machine in the watch-room at the fire station, which is manned twenty-four hours. Mr Murrant told the reporter that the public has used the street alarms about a dozen times in the last year, but most calls they receive these days (1954) come by telephone. He asked the public that if you pull the handle in the alarm box, then please wait for the fire engine to arrive.

There are fifteen special fire telephones installed in glass-fronted boxes with direct contact to the fire station. They are in the town's hospitals, entertainment houses and other places where many people congregate. The brigade checks each of these boxes twice a day.

With recent upgrading of Eastbourne Fire Brigade, the council promoted Deputy Chief Fire Officer P. C. Short to a new position of Assistant Divisional Officer at a salary of £802 a year. This was with effect from1 October 1954.

Another tragic event took place in January 1955 when senior fire officer, Chief Fire Officer Charles J. Murrant, aged only 46, passed away. He died suddenly at his home in Old Orchard Road, on Friday the 14th, of a blood clot which reached his heart. They held the funeral on Thursday, 20 January, at All Souls' Church.

Mr Murrant joined the fire service in 1926 as a volunteer fireman, and in September 1953, became Chief Fire Officer in Eastbourne. Representatives from the Council, Eastbourne Police and the Fire Service, together with family and friends, attended the church service. Also, at the service were Chief Fire Officers from six fire brigades along with members from the St. John Ambulance and a representative from the Home Office. The newspapers reported that over five hundred people attended the service. Afterwards, the family conveyed the coffin to Brighton for cremation. During the service, the brigade received a call out. This was to attend a chimney fire, and as most of the Eastbourne firefighters were at the church, the East Sussex Brigade helped to subdue the fire.

With the death of Mr Murrant, the Home Office in February contacted Eastbourne Council. They suggested that as per the Fire Service Act 1947, the council should consider amalgamating its fire services with the East Sussex Fire Service. The Watch Committee arranged for three representatives from Eastbourne to contact East Sussex County Council to discuss the matter. The local newspapers carried many comments from residents supporting Eastbourne's independent Borough fire service. In the meantime, the council were still looking for a suitable applicant for the position of Chief Fire Officer. Also, in February, the brigade attended a large fire at the bakery in Church Street, Old Town and took delivery of a new Bedford Water tender and 35ft ladder.

"Man Leaps from Blazing House" was a headline in April. Michael Mardon alias 'Cuthbert the Clown' escaped death after jumping from the second floor of his house, The Hoo, Church Street, Willingdon. A passing police patrol car spotted the fire and immediately notified the Eastbourne fire service. On arrival, they found Mr Mardon on the ground, bruised, burned and bleeding. He had severe injuries to his hands and head, and they took him to hospital. Deputy Chief Fire Officer Short was soon on scene with a pump escape, a water tender and an emergency tender. With firefighters in breathing apparatus, they soon brought the fire under control. Whilst the Eastbourne firemen were fighting the blaze, an appliance and pump arrived from Hailsham, followed shortly after by an East Sussex Fire Brigade officer who had travelled by car from Bexhill.

Mr Mardon, educated at Harrow and born in the West Country in 1919, later went to Cambridge as a student but decided in 1946 to join the circus. In 1961 he wrote a book about his adventures.

Following the death of Mr Murrant, they advertised the position of Chief Fire Officer in the press and according to the *Eastbourne Herald Chronicle* of the 2 April, sixty-six applicants applied for the job. The candidates were mainly Deputy Chief Fire Officers from around the country. They ranged from Hastings district to Blackpool, in Lancashire. They eventually offered the position to assistant Divisional Officer, Mr P. C. Short, although he would not take up his position for some months.

In the same newspaper, they announced an increase in pay for firemen. A Leading Fireman would receive £10 17s a week, an increase of 10s, a sub-Officer £12 2s up from £11 7s. And a Station Officer £772 a year increased from £742.

Pat Charles Short

I.M. INSPECTOR S. H. CHARTERS and the Mayor chat with one of the firemen during Tuesday's inspection. See page 5.

E/B Chronicle 4 June 1955

Mr S. H. Charters the H.M. Inspector of Brigades, and Mayor, Councillor L. W. Pyle carried out the annual brigade inspection in June. This was the first time Mr Charters had visited Eastbourne, and he complimented the parade on a good turnout and the precision of the drills.

In Maresfield, they held a Firemen Drill competition in July, and East Sussex Fire Brigade invited a five-man team from Eastbourne Auxiliary Fire Brigade to participate. They were under the command of Sub-Officer E. Thorne and won second place in the featherweight pump exercise.

"Eastbourne Against Fire Brigades merger" was the headline in the *Eastbourne Herald* in the October 1st issue. The Watch Committee advised the Town Council that after many meetings they did not favour the amalgamation of the two brigades. Their decision was unanimous. They would inform the Home Office and East Sussex County Council of their decision. They also agreed they would supply the Eastbourne brigade with six hundred feet of hose for the year 1955-1956. The cost of this would be one hundred pounds.

At the Town Council meeting in early October. They agreed to pay Fire Officer Short an additional allowance.

This was to equal the difference of his pay between Deputy and Chief Fire Officer. As he was now temporarily taking on the job as Chief. The Council would backdate this to the 1ˢᵗ of April.

Many years ago, the Eastbourne Fire Brigade won an individual competition cup, which received severe damage when the bomb hit the Grove Road fire station in 1943. They have recently repaired the cup, and they presented it to the winners of October's Watch Drills Competition. Teams of fireman are always very competitive when attending drills and this year two Watches shared the cup.

Red and Blue Watch drew in the competition they held in the station yard and shared the trophy. Deputy Chief Officer, Mr Short remarked at the presentation "This shows that for one year at least the two watches are equal". In the first drill, Blue Watch beat Red Watch by four seconds carrying the telescopic escape to the third floor of the escape tower and rescuing a 'trapped person'. The next task was to rescue someone from the fourth floor with the aid of hook ladders. Red Watch won this competition by two seconds. The last event was a water tender drill, which resulted in a draw. After a volleyball match, which Red Watch won, they invited everyone into the reception room where the Mayor presented the Queen's Long Service Medals to Station Officer Scarlett and six other members of the brigade.

There had been concerns in the brigade about delays caused by the level crossing in Hampden Park. Often an appliance would have to wait for the gates to open, which could cause delay and a fatality at a fire. There were now more houses being built on the east of the railway line, and the Fire Officers decided to seek a solution to this problem. In 1954 they arranged that when called for, they would send two appliances to Hampden Park. One would use the regular route, and they would send the other one via Seaside and Lottbridge Drove.

Late in November 1955, they put the new scheme into operation and proved it a success. After receiving a call to a fire at The Hydneye, a street in Hampden Park, the first engine responded. This engine got delayed at the level crossing gates. The second engine travelled by the alternate route. Although the journey to the incident was three-tenths of a mile longer, the second engine arrived at the fire, four minutes before the first. The Fire Officers were pleased with the operation of their new plan.

The Borough received a reply from the Home Office in January 1956, advising they had accepted Eastbourne's decision not to merge with the East Sussex Fire Service. The Council had seen no advantage or material financial gain with the two brigades joining forces. They could now confirm Mr Short as the new Chief Fire Officer. Also, the Watch Committee decided that all members of the Eastbourne Fire Brigade would be examined in first-aid. The St John Ambulance Brigade would carry out these tests at £9 9s per member.

March was hectic for the firemen, and one of the busiest times they have had.

The Council appointed Station Officer R. A. Scarlett as Deputy Chief Fire Officer. The brigade reported over seventeen call outs in one weekend and several more in the following days. They considered only a few were serious. There was also one false alarm and one burst water pipe. This was a testing time for the new Chief Fire Officer.

The headline from the *Eastbourne Herald Chronicle* of the 31 March read "Firemen working too long hours, says Union". The Fire Brigades Union stated this issue is causing "grave concern" as they continue discussions with council officers. The Union wanted a 56-hour week and a three-shift duty system for the firefighters. At present, the men were working a 60-hour week, and as shifts changed on Sunday, this meant that they could work a consecutive day and night shift. The Council did not want to change the present system. It was pointed out to them by the Fire Brigade Union that twenty-two County Boroughs had adopted this scheme. The Council held a second meeting with the National Association of Fire Officers who had thought the idea workable. But the Council said it would contact other County Boroughs before reaching a conclusion.

Fireman E. Guy had recently received a promotion to the temporary position of Leading Fireman. In May, the Chief Fire Officer recommended they should promote him to Sub-Officer. This was to maintain a satisfactory working balance of junior officers on each Watch. He asked the Council to approve his appointment, which they agreed.

At another meeting of the Watch Committee in June, they authorised the removal of the public fire alarm system. It was now twenty-five years since its installation. In the past, the public used the system reasonably well, but now it had become outdated. Chief Fire Officer Mr Short gave this information to the Committee and informed them that most calls came from telephone boxes or private homes these days. The system was costing the service about £115 a year with £50 for maintenance.

They also announced at the meeting that the Council and Fire Brigades Union had reached an agreement. The Council offered a 58-hour working week, which the Union accepted. This would come into effect at once.

Reported in the local newspapers in June that from 1st July the street fire alarm system would be out of commission. The public could receive help if they made a call from the nearest telephone or police boxes.

There was a special presentation by the chairman of the Watch Committee, Alderman, Commander A. L. D. Skinner on the 7 September at the retirement party for Fireman Frank L. Taylor. His colleagues had subscribed for a clock to be presented to Mr Taylor to mark his retirement after twenty-five years of service. After serving fifteen years in the Royal Navy, in 1931 he joined the Eastbourne fire service. During World War II he was recalled and returned to the brigade in 1949. Chief Fire Officer P. Short said that he was extremely sorry to lose Fireman Taylor and "He has proved himself a very able and efficient man".

Mr Taylor is the first fireman to retire from the Eastbourne Brigade since the re-organisation in 1931.

E/B Gazette 12 September 1956

On the 1st October after forty-two years' service, another fireman retires. Harry Payne, a carpenter by trade, followed in his father's footsteps and joined the fire service in 1914. He was called up at the outbreak of World War I and served in the Royal Engineers in Flanders. After hostilities finished, he returned to Eastbourne and the fire service. Now at the age of 62, he said, "I feel it is a young man's job". During his service he had attended some of the worst fires that Eastbourne experienced. The three that stand out in his memory are the fires at All Saints' Church, the Marine Laundry and Pearson's in South Street. Mr Payne is also a holder of the Queen's medal for long service. On Friday the 5th on behalf of members of the Eastbourne Fire Brigade there was a presentation made by Chief Fire Officer Short. Mr Payne received a clock inscribed with his record of service.

At a meeting of the Finance Committee in December. The Watch Committee advised they would buy a new car for the fire service. The cost of this would £675 plus £100 for its equipment.

February 1957 and Chief Fire Officer Mr Short gave a talk to the Young Women's Christian Association, Young Wives, when he reported that the brigade received 488 calls to fires last year. The highest number they had received since 1941.

He informed the gathering that until 1931 the service was a volunteer service. After the re-organisation they were now a permanent service and that the service now costs £23,000 a year to maintain. They collect this expense from the rate-payers and "that a five-penny rate covers the cost". He reassured the audience that they fully staff the fire station both night and day. At night two men were on duty whilst their colleagues slept until they received a call. Then he gave a few hints on fire prevention before answering questions from the meeting.

In the financial report from the Watch Committee for the year ending 31 March 1957, they confirmed that there were forty-one full-time and ten retained firemen in the service. Supported by forty-five AFS members. Based on the average daily strength, the cost per man was £696 8s 5d a year. The Chief Fire Officer confirmed they attended 488 calls of which 26 were from outside the borough. They also received six malicious false alarms during the year. Morale in the brigade was improved knowing that the brigade will stay under borough control. He confirmed that there were 1,832 fire hydrants in the borough with the water supplies from the Eastbourne Waterworks Company. The v.h.f radio equipment was working well, and liaison with the police was operating efficiently.

They received seventy-one calls during the year from the police and the fire prevention department made 962 inspections of various businesses. They had given preliminary firefighting training to the Boy Scouts and Girl Guides and twenty-eight members of the police.

Mr F Dann, the Home Office Inspector, carried out his annual inspection of the brigade in March. The Deputy Mayor, Chief Fire Officer and Chairman of the Watch Committee accompanied him. This was the eighth time he had inspected the local fire service, and he reported that he had always found the men and equipment to be in first-class order. During his visit, the Deputy Mayor presented Fireman A. Carey with a twenty years' Long Service medal.

In July and the town received a deluge of thunder, lightning and rain. It rained for over five hours, hailstones, thunder and water came pouring down from the skies. It flooded the streets and shops. The brigade received 150 calls for help in pumping out premises. They cancelled all leave and spent all day and night trying to restore the situation. It had rained from a little after 4 a.m. until 9.30 a.m. The storm deposited over two-and-a-half inches of water on the town and telephone lines were out of action. In Motcombe district there was an electricity failure, which they repaired after an hour and a half. Flooding affected shops, factories and the brewery and they estimated that the Plummer's drapery store in Terminus Road lost over £10,000 of stock from their downstairs showroom.

They held a Christmas party on Saturday 11 January 1958 at the fire station for the wives and children of the brigade. About forty children attended a gathering in the station messroom, which the firemen had decorated with bunting and a Christmas tree. First, there were cartoon films, followed by games and the singing of carols.

Mrs H. Pinfield, the brigade's cook, made sandwiches, cakes, jellies and mince pies for the party tea. Naturally, Santa Claus, retired fireman Mr H. Payne, made an appearance and presented a toy to each boy and girl. Some children did not attend the party because of illness, and they sent their presents to their homes. The social club sub-committee organised the party. In the evening members of the brigade and their wives had their party.

Three chimney fires in one week and then the worst fire since the end of the war. Local residents on Thursday 23 January were awakened by the crackle of flames and discovered a fire shortly after 5.00 a.m. in South Street. Mr E. Pounds, who lived nearby and an employee of Messrs Pinker ran across the road to the police station. They immediately notified the fire brigade. By the time four fire engines arrived on the scene, the flames were 30ft above the building. The premise was the business of wholesale greengrocer F. R. Pinker Ltd at 2a South Street behind the New Hotel. They had suffered a large fire in their warehouse just before Christmas in December 1951. Other businesses affected were a piano tuner and the repair shop of Dobie, Reeves and Dobie. The police closed South Street to enable the firefighters to tackle the blaze and they did not re-open the street until 8 a.m.

The firemen connected five hose lines and used hydrants in Furness Road and South Street. With very little wind blowing, they brought the fire under control within an hour. There were no casualties except for Fireman Wooller when a falling slate from the roof struck his hand. The fire gutted the building, and the blaze destroyed stock, two lorries and several pianos. It also destroyed an entire block of shops and business premises, with the damage estimated at £13,000. Firemen remained on the scene during Thursday, damping down the embers.

The brigade had their annual inspection on 25 March by Mr Dann from the Home Office. All the men turned out in their well-polished buttons and uniforms except for four firemen who were out on a call.

This was to a chimney fire in Green Street which took them one and a quarter-hour to extinguish. They arrived on parade a little dusty and dishevelled.

One fireman, C. Suter, arrived in the nick of time to receive his Queen's Fire Service, Long Service and Good Conduct medals. This was for serving twenty years in the brigade. Station Officer A. Green also received a twenty years of service medal from the Mayor who presented the medals.

Shortly after, Chief Fire Officer Short presented his annual report to the Committee. He had an article in the local paper stating that there had been 541 fires reported in the last year. Of these, he maintained carelessness caused twenty-five of the fires, unattended appliances caused a further nine. Sparks from fires, over-heating of fat and bonfires were also a major concern. He reminded everyone to be more aware of fire and try to avoid accidents in the home. There were no malicious false alarms reported during the year, although there had been six in the previous year. Recruitment for the Auxiliary Fire Service was still a problem with only five new enrolments during the year.

On a lighter note, Chief Fire Officer Pat Short and his wife hosted an evening for the wives and children of members of the fire brigade. They held the entertainment at Bourne Street station with over eighty people attending, and everyone enjoyed the show. There were firemen demonstrating rescues, and amusing sketches performed by colleagues. Afterwards, they served tea, ice cream and refreshments before they all departed.

In the Queen's Birthday Honours, reported in the *Eastbourne Herald* 14 June, four local people received honours. One of these was the Chief Fire Officer Short. They awarded him with the Queen's Fire Service Medal. He had been a fireman since September 1931 and served his entire career in Eastbourne. A formal ceremony took place at Brighton Fire Brigade Headquarters on 23 September 1958, when the Lord Lieutenant of Sussex, the Duke of Norfolk, made the presentation.

A worrying time for Chief Fire Officer Short and his wife when they, at last, received a reassuring letter from their twenty-year-old son, Tony. The family had not heard from him in over three weeks. Their son was serving as a radio operator with the RAF and stationed in Habbaniya in Iraq. On 14 July, there was a coup d'état in Iraq which resulted in the overthrow of the Hashemite monarchy. Rebel Iraqi troops had taken over the radio station his son was in, and the base placed under a curfew from 10 p.m. till 5 a.m. He informed them not to worry and that he was O.K.

"Five killed" was in the headline of the *Eastbourne Gazette* of 27 August as they reported on "the worst tragedy in the peacetime history of Eastbourne". Early on Monday the 25th August, the Glasgow Car-Sleeper Express, a steam train crashed into the 7.25 a.m., a twelve-coach electric passenger train.

The train waiting on platform 4 was departing from Eastbourne for London Bridge station and was seven minutes late in departure. It was the Ore-London Bridge regular commuter train, locally known as the 'friendly train'. Most of the travellers used to travel every day together on this service and knew each other's first names.

There was a delay of nearly half an hour before the Eastbourne fire crews attended the accident at 7.58 a.m., and they worked for many hours dealing with the wreckage. A misunderstanding at the police station regarding the correct procedure caused the delay. Assistance also came from the Eastbourne County Borough Transport Department, who made available their oxy-acetylene cutting plant and breakdown vehicle, equipped with tools, and jacks.

The front two carriages from the electric train mounted the Glasgow express, which then crashed into a signal gantry. The rear carriage hit the platform buffers. There was only one casualty in the steam train who had minor injuries; the train driver and fireman suffered from shock. The driver of the electric train, Mr Cyril Brock, from St. Leonards, was not so lucky and lost his life.

There was only one passenger in the first carriage of the electric train and very few in the second.

This was usually a six-carriage train. Otherwise, the death total would have been much higher.

E/B Gazette 27 August 1958

Removing wreckage after fatal crash.

Two of Glasgow's train carriages telescoped together, but fortunately, these were the car carriages. One was badly shattered, but the Jaguar sports car inside escaped damage.

The Glasgow train had departed at 7.47 p.m. with thirty-six passengers and eleven cars. In total, five people, four men and one woman, all on the Eastbourne train, lost their lives. Forty-one other passengers were injured, with five detained in Princess Alice Hospital.

In the report by Colonel W. P. Reed, the Inspector of Railways, published in March 1959. He criticised the crew of the steam train for passing a danger signal. Although there was heavy rain at the time, with restricted visibility, the report stated the train was still travelling at an excessive speed. Sussex Assizes subsequently tried the train driver, Alfred Wembridge for manslaughter, but acquitted him of all charges. Although the rail report stated that he "must accept full responsibility for the accident".

Another view of the train crash wreckage.

At the annual inspection of the brigade on 17 March by Mr Dann from the Home Office, they awarded two Long Service medals. The Mayor presented one to Fireman C. Cranch and the other to Fireman S. Ellis for completing twenty years' service.

On 30 May, the Eastbourne brigade attended a fire at the Watling RAF station, where they assisted the Herstmonceux and Pevensey brigades. They confined the fire and consequent damage to the switchgear at the station. A few weeks later they were called back again to another small blaze at the RAF station.

In the local newspaper on 17 June, they reported that at a recent meeting of the Watch Committee, Chief Fire Officer Short advised them that after interviewing six applicants he had appointed two firewomen to join the brigade. He appointed Mrs Annie K. Long as a firewoman, and she would start her duties on 8 June; Miss Jacqueline Burton would start as a junior firewoman on the 22 June.

The local Fire Brigades Union had objected to women being employed to undertake watch room duties, but the committee recommended that the appointments be approved.

Most fires are extinguished within hours if not minutes of their discovery. But sometimes there are large and difficult blazes for the brigade to tackle. One such was in Willingdon in mid-June 1959, where for four days and almost non-stop, the brigade fought a fire in a Dutch barn on Brodricklands Farm. The Eastbourne Fire Brigade received the call about the outbreak on Friday afternoon. They were told that 200 tons of baled hay had caught fire.

With the help of an appliance from Hailsham, they fought the blaze continuously day and night, and it was not until Monday afternoon when they finally put out the fire.

On 23 June, Fireman Ronald Simmonds was responding to a 'shout' to a fire at the Corporation rubbish tip. After turning out of Southbourne Road into Seaside, he stopped by Vine Square. A motorcycle with a pillion passenger then collided with his fire tender. They took the motorcyclist suffering from a concussion to the hospital.

In court, Fireman Simmonds started he had indicated his intention to turn left and saw the motorcycle approaching him at an estimated speed of 40 miles per hour. He told the court he had been driving for twenty-five years, and this was his first summons. The motorcyclist could not recall the incident and was not required to give evidence to the court. Some witnesses came forward and gave evidence about the accident. After considering the matter, Eastbourne Magistrate's Court found Fireman Simmonds not guilty of driving without due care.

Patrick Smith

AFS at Bourne Street with Fordson 7v appliance.

William Dancey

In December 1964, Chief Fire Officer Pat Short resigned from the service, and William F. Dancey succeeded him.

Known as Bill, he joined the Eastbourne Brigade from Gloucester in 1962, aged 37 and served as Deputy Chief Fire Officer. After just three years as Chief Fire Officer, he resigned his post and accepted the position of Chief Fire Officer of the Swansea Brigade. With the government re-organisation in 1974, he became Chief Fire Officer for the newly created West Glamorgan Fire Brigade.

The sixty-year-old single-storey Beachy Head Hotel owned by Vintage Inns Ltd had recently received a £60,000 face-lift. When early Wednesday morning on 6 April 1966 a disastrous fire broke out. A farmworker saw smoke coming from the roof of the building at 6.30 a.m. and raised the alarm. By the time three fire engines reached the hotel, it had already sustained considerable damage. The firemen had problems with water supply, and with powerful winds blowing, they could not save the hotel. They reported at the time that flames leapt 50ft into the air. Fortunately, there were no casualties. After dampening down, all that remained of the hotel were the chimney stacks and the fireplace in the restaurant.

E/B Chronicle 6 April 1966

In January 1967, the brigade bought a Merryweather turntable 100ft ladder. It was on an A.E.C chassis and had the registration number DHC 222 E. They later sold this in 1990 as the brigade was having problems getting spares.

Britain's biggest-ever oil spill occurred off the coast in Cornwall on 18 March 1967. The SS *Torrey Canyon*, a Suezmax Class oil tanker, was on her way from Kuwait to a refinery at Milford Haven in Wales.

She ran aground on Pollard's Rock on the Seven Stones Reef between the Isles of Scilly and Land's End in Cornwall. Splitting her tanks that held some of her vast cargo of crude oil. Over 120,000 tonnes of oil spilt into the sea. And this polluted the beaches in the south and west of Cornwall. A call went out for volunteers, and 150 fire brigades from around the country responded and travelled down to help.

On Wednesday 12 April, the first detachment of forty firemen from the South Coast area departed for Cornwall. There were two officers together with colleagues from Kent, Hastings, Brighton and East Sussex Brigades. Eastbourne Fire Brigade provided four of their men.

Another major incident for the Eastbourne Fire Brigade happened on the evening of 20 October 1968 off the coast at Holywell. The vessel, the Norwegian *Sitakund*, a 15,567 tonnes oil tanker, was sailing from Wilhelmshaven, Germany to Libya. She had recently discharged her cargo, and the crew had not properly vented her cargo tanks of flammable gases. Men were working in the tanks cleaning them. And this was most likely the reason for the two large explosions that occurred. The first explosion at about 20.00 hours split open the ship's inch thick steel plating on her main deck above the centre tanks. This was on both the port and starboard

E/B Gazette 23 October 1968
Meeching alongside *Sitakund*.

side of the vessel. The ensuing fire spread to the engine room, stores and crew's quarters, and there was the possibility of further explosions.

At the time she was sailing around seventeen miles off Beachy Head. Newspapers reported that people could hear the blasts of the explosions from Newhaven across to Pevensey Bay and Bexhill. Thirty-one members of the crew got into lifeboats and rowed towards a French trawler that had come to assist. (A group of French trawlers were first on the scene and not long after joined by the Royal Navy frigate H.M.S. *Mohawk*.)

The trawler fishermen then transferred the crew to the *Mohawk*, which had been diverted to give any assistance she could. She was sailing from Portsmouth to Rosyth, Fife, and took the crew of the *Sitakund* to the Royal Naval Hospital in Haslar, Gosport.

Three sailors on the *Sitakund,* unfortunately, died in the first explosion. One of these was Mr Joseph Knowles, aged 42, from Hebburn, Co Durham. The Captain Ole D. Terjesen and six of the crew stayed on board to extinguish the flames, even though there was still a threat of further explosions. An aircraft chartered by a local Eastbourne newspaper flew over the ship and reported that they could see a three-mile oil trail in the ship's wake.

The skipper, Captain Alec Pringle of the 170-ton British Railways tug *Meeching*, moored in Newhaven, received instructions to attend the stricken vessel. He was to aid in the fire and help recovery. They got a man and a line aboard and towed the vessel to Eastbourne Bay. At 21.00 hours, instructions were given to launch both the Eastbourne and Newhaven lifeboats to give assistance and look for missing crewmen.

Jim Dunstan

Dominant and Meeching attending Sitakund.

Fortunately, because of favourable winds and tides, there was no danger to Eastbourne's beaches. Also involved in the incident was the Dover based tug *Dominant*. It and the *Meeching* managed to ground the *Sitakund* on rocks a little west of Dukes Mound.

Eastbourne's firemen were called to assist early on Monday morning after receiving a call from the Sussex Police. Using the pier as a staging point, the *Irene*, a local fishing boat, helped in ferrying the firefighters out to the still blazing ship. The *Dominant* and the *Meeching* crews finally put out the fire, assisted with a water monitor mounted on top of the tug's wheelhouse.

Initially, they transferred ten firemen, Chief Fire Officer Dancey and Deputy Fire Officers with equipment out to the *Sitakund*. The men fought the blaze for some days. It was not until Tuesday afternoon when they considered it was safe to retrieve two bodies from the ship. The firemen requested extra foam early on Wednesday, and at 1600 hrs they received a 'stop' message and fire crews could then stand down. When they had extinguished the blaze, the tugs tried to refloat the ship, but that was impossible. Eastbourne's lifeboat *Beryl Tollemache* played a large part in the day's activities. After seventeen hours on duty by the stricken tanker, the lifeboat was called upon to ferry extra supplies for the firefighters. The lifeboat was on duty for twenty hours after launching at 8.45 on Sunday evening and returning to shore about five o'clock.

Mr Dancey, in October, submitted his report on the fire to Eastbourne County Borough.

Eventually, the Folkstone Salvage Company cut the ship into two parts and successfully refloated the forward section of the tanker in December 1968. The tug *Englishman* towed it to Falmouth. A few months later, they towed the rest of the wreckage away to Spain. They would return to salvage the anchor and chain in a few days.

Frank Tarling

After the retirement of Chief Fire Officer W. F. Dancey in October 1968, the Watch Committee appointed Mr Frank Tarling as the new Chief Fire Officer. He was formally the Deputy Chief Fire Officer of the Oxford Fire Brigade. And would become the last Chief Fire Officer of the Eastbourne Fire Brigade.

In August 1969, a new fire engine was ordered. Sir Sidney Caffyn, Alderman, former Mayor, and director of the Caffyn motor dealership, gifted a 50ft hydraulic platform to the Brigade. It was on a Bedford TK with HCB bodywork. The Bedford served for several years and by 1988 was listed as out of service.

About 2.00 p.m. on Thursday, 8 January 1970, Mr Dick Griffin, the assistant Pier Master, and Mr D. J. Strutt while working in the auditorium, discovered a fire in the 1000 seat Starlight Theatre. Two GPO engineers, Mr Ernest Smith and Mr M. D. Ward were laying telephone cables on the pier when they also noticed smoke billowing from the theatre roof. Mr Smith immediately raised the alarm by smashing the glass and pulling the handle in a nearby fire alarm box. They then got two of the pier's fire hoses and their ladders and fought the fire themselves.

The fire station received the call, and the first appliance arrived at the pier within ten minutes. The Eastbourne Brigade led by Chief Fire Office Tarling initially despatched four appliances to attend the blaze. This was a big fire with on-shore winds fanning the flames. Within fifteen minutes of the firefighters arriving, the ceiling above the stage collapsed, and it soon became clear to Mr Tarling that they needed assistance from neighbouring fire stations. He requested help from the East Sussex Fire Brigade. They responded by sending crews and one engine from Bexhill. Pevensey, Hailsham, Lewes, Herstmonceux and Burwash fire stations also responded. The Seaford Brigade stood on standby. Whilst waiting for more men to arrive, pier staff, assisted firefighters and some pier staff operated water jets. At 2.40 p.m., one of the two pagoda towers of the theatre at the shore side collapsed. Its partner tower followed shortly afterwards. They then closed the pier to the public. By this time, sizable crowds of shoppers and residents crowded the seafront to watch. They soon dispersed when at 3.30 p.m., there was a shower of hailstones followed by snow which strong winds blew across the pier.

The area of the seafront road was a maze of hoses with hydrants along the seafront and outside the Queens Hotel being used. There were six lines of fire hoses stretching along the pier attached to the fire appliances at the pier entrance. By 4.40 p.m., the firemen had the blaze under control. When a reporter interviewed Chief Fire Officer Tarling, he said that "fortunately the safety curtain was down when the fire broke out", "that saved the rest of the building".

The pier, designed by Eugenius Birch, and built in the 1870s, was 300 meters long. They built the structure on stilts which rest in cups on the seabed. At the height of the fire, sixty firefighters, some wearing breathing apparatus, fought the blaze. Strong on-shore winds gutted the main stage and the dressing room area. The fire destroyed the wardrobe and theatrical stores. It also destroyed the old clock and the stairs leading to the camera obscura.

Active firefighting operations went on until 10.00 p.m. on Thursday with two members of Eastbourne Fire Brigade on watch duty throughout the night. No firemen sustained any serious injury, with the only casualty, Mr Griffin. They took him to hospital with smoke inhalation, but he soon returned to the pier to help fight the fire.

A few days later the police charged a stagehand worker, David John Strutt with "unlawfully and maliciously" setting the fire. He ignited the fire with used rags and paraffin, which he placed under the stage. The pier company had only employed him three weeks earlier. On the 16 March, Strutt pleaded guilty to setting two fires on the pier. And at Sussex Assizes in Lewes, they sentenced him to be "detained during her Majesty's pleasure at Broadmoor". This was not the first, nor would it be the last fire to occur on the pier.

It was back in 1965 when the Fire Brigade and the Licensing Committees first considered Lewes Road would be a suitable site for a new fire station. But after much discussion, they chose the Whitley Road site. The Borough Council eventually approved plans in 1969 to erect the new fire headquarters building in Whitley Road. This was on the site of the Stafford County Junior School, which had previously been the site of the Bedfordwell C.E. Secondary and St. Philip's C.E. Infants Schools.

The council instructed Mr J. Connolly, the Borough Architect, to draw up plans and send them to the Council. They arranged to send out advertisements for tenders for the works. In 1971 they reached an agreement with E. Powell & Sons Limited about the costs for the new fire station. He had submitted the lowest tender at £188,909.

We should remember that back in early 1899, Captain Hounsom first suggested that they should build a new fire station in Whitley Road.

At last, it was going to happen.

Construction on the one-acre ground for the new building started in January 1972, and they laid the foundation stone on 20 April 1972. The Mayor, Councillor John Robinson with the H.M. Inspector of Fire Brigades, Mr G. R. H. Payne conducted the ceremony and inspected forty members of the brigade and their five fire appliances.

On the 4 Dec 1973, the Duke of Norfolk, Lord Lieutenant of Sussex, performed the official opening together with the Mayor, Sir Sydney Caffyn and the H.M. Inspector of Fire Brigades.

The building which faced Whitley Road had space for six fire appliances and a two-bay workshop. On the ground floor, there were offices, a conference room, a messroom and kitchen. The upper floor accommodated more offices together with a dormitory/restroom with a television and study room. In the yard, there is a fifty-foot drill and hose drying tower and extra space for storing equipment.

This building was the new headquarters for the Eastbourne Fire Brigade. But within weeks everything would change with the local government reforms, together with the reorganisation of the Sussex fire service on the 1 April 1974. This brought about many changes. And so, after a hundred and fifty years ended the Eastbourne Borough's responsibility for its fire service.

They merged the brigades of Brighton, Eastbourne, East Sussex and Hastings. These now form part of the East Sussex Fire Brigade under the control of Chief Fire Officer Dawn Whittaker and the authority of East Sussex County Council. Some changes moved control of some East Sussex fire stations into the West Sussex area. All brigades in East Sussex now come under the name of East Sussex Fire and Rescue Service with their headquarters in Lewes. On 7 April 1975, the watch room at Eastbourne was closed. All 999 calls and mobilising of appliances were now the responsibility of the centralised brigade.

****

LAST DAY COVER
31st March, 1974. Cessation of the County Borough of
Eastbourne Fire Brigade

Sold in aid of the Fire Services National Benevolent Fund

No. 148

THE PHILATELIC OFFICER,
FIRE STATION,
EASTBOURNE

9 FIRE STATIONS

Grove Road. 1851 – 1902

The original 'fire station' in Grove Road was at the Vestry Hall, which a local business owner John Haine, in 1851, paid for its construction. It had cost £270 to build and in July 1896 became the library. By 1857 they decided there was a need for new premises, and they constructed Eastbourne's first purpose-built fire station. This cost eighty pounds. It was known as the Parish Engine House and stood roughly opposite the entrance to Ivy Terrace.

In later years the firemen complained the building was damp and causing concern, so towards the end of 1902, the Vestry demolished the building. This was to make way for the fresh development of the New Technical Institute, Free Library and a new Fire Station.

Market House. 1903 – 1906

Between 1902 and 1906, after they demolished the old station and waiting for their new fire station, the crews and equipment moved into the old Market House in Grove Road. The building was only being used for storage, and the council leased the premises from Mr William Hudson. The brigade would use half of the building, and the Free Library with a reading room used the other half. This would be a temporary home for the fire service and library until they completed the new building.

Grove Road   1906 – 1943

"Fire and Water" January 1906

Architect Mr P. A. Robson deigned the new station, and Messrs Peerless Dennis & Co. of Langney Road. built it There had been sixteen bidders for the contract, with prices quoted from £4659 to £5423. Messrs Peerless Dennis & Co won the contract for the new red brick building at an agreed price of £4,768. Work began in January 1906 and the Mayor, Alderman S. N. Fox officially opened the new fire station on Saturday 3 November. Besides the local councillors, representatives from Sussex and Kent's brigades and the fireman's union attended the ceremony.

The building, a two-storey structure with a covered 65ft by 23ft drill yard at the back had an engine house, 32ft by 20ft and fitted with quick-opening doors supplied by Shand Mason. There was space to house a Steamer and a Manual engine, plus fire escape and hose reels. At the back, there was another entrance for returning engines to enter.

Besides offices and the watch room, there was a sizeable recreation room, 30ft by 14ft, for the firefighters to rest. Also, a bathroom attached. On the first floor were three bedrooms, a sitting room, a kitchen and a bathroom. At the rear was a 6ft square, 45ft high hose-tower. This again was in red brick and lighted on each side.

In case of an emergency, there was now a caretaker stationed in the building twenty-fours a day. In the basement was a large storeroom which the Corporation electricity department occasionally used.

In 1928/32 there were alterations to the building, and they added a floor, giving space for a further seven rooms and an extra bay for a fire engine. On the first and second floor they converted some rooms into residential flats for two brigade families. The photo below shows the building on the left that was used as the electricity showroom

The fire station was destroyed in February 1943 when a bomb hit the station and killed six firefighters. Five men and one woman. That was the end of fire stations in Grove Road.

February 1943

Front view of bombed Grove Road Fire Station

14 Langney Road. 1876 – 1884

The station known as the Central Fire Station had no connection with the Vestry, and their fire engine was privately owned. This private brigade comprised of twelve men, a hose cart and other small appliances. Their first appliance was a Manual engine bought from Merryweather & Co. But within eighteen months, they decided they needed a more powerful Steamer engine and exchanged their Manual for a Steamer. The brigade named this new engine the "Fire King". This horse drawn Steamer had been exhibited by Merryweather & Co recently and should not be confused with the motor fire engine that Merryweather called the "Fire King".

According to a report in the local newspaper on 2 April 1884, they removed the Steam fire engine from the Parish Engine House. They took it to Mr C. Bradford's, stables in Royal Victoria Mews. As Mr Bradford was a council member, this arrangement could only be temporary. The council were considering utilising premises in Vine Place. But there was no quick way of calling the crews together as Grove Road station only had telephone connection with four men. It was suggested that the council should decide quickly about the fate of the Steam engine. Mr Fuller, who was in charge of this private brigade, and after many conversations with the council, built a new fire station. This was the Cavendish Place fire station. They demolished the Langney Road building in the 1920s.

52b Cavendish Place. 1885 - 1933 in use 1941-1944

Mr Fuller built this brick building with a slatted roof. Constructed as a purpose-built fire station, he offered it to the council in Oct 1885. After much discussion with the council, they agreed to rent the building for fourteen years. In September 1896, the council asked the Local Government Board for a loan to enable them to buy Cavendish Road Fire Station as they were paying rent on the premises and the lease was about to expire. Mr Fuller had offered the council the freehold for nine hundred pounds. The Council agreed to purchase and by March the following year, the Town Clerk confirmed they had completed the purchase.

With the reorganisation of the fire service in the 1930s, the council decided that Cavendish Road fire station was no longer required.

Records in March 1933 show that Messrs Willing and Co Ltd leased the building for seven years at a rent of £60 p.a.

During WW2 the National Fire Service reopened the building as a fire station again. In the 50s-60s, Harris Builders had their business there. Later the building because of disuse became derelict. They demolished the empty building in 2012.

As far back as March 1899, there were suggestions they should sell the fire station in Cavendish Place and build a new one in Whitley Road.

5 Watts Lane.   1889 – 1940

The hose reel and fire station were built by William & John R. Newman and leased it to the council for seven years at a rent of £12 per year.

48 Meads Street.   1899 – 1934

The Building Surveyor submitted plans to the Watch Committee on 26 March

1897 with full specifications for the new fire station. This was after years of residents demanding fire cover for the Meads area.

Finally, the Watch Committee in August 1897 agreed to purchase land offered at £195 from the Compton Place Estates. They invited tenders for the erection of a new fire station and accepted the one from Mr J. C. Lacey of £575.

They built the station in 1898, and used it to house the Manual fire pump, which used to be at Grove Road Station. (1919).

The new fire station had a hose drying tower at the back, and the fire officer used the cottage at the rear. According to records, they sold the building on 31 October 1934 to William and Emily Gertrude Midson for £1.200. Mr Midson then opened the premises as a motor garage.

Hampden Park. 1911 – 1932

The fire station was in Railway Road, now renamed Elm Grove, and was next to the electricity sub-station. This was just a small station with just four firemen attending. Originally, they used a small hand-cart to carry their equipment and a ladder, and they attired the men with blue shirts and flat sailor type hats. They later supplied the men with more up-to-date equipment. The fire station closed on 30 April 1932.

8 Southfields Road. 1943 – 1946

E/B Gazette 20 March 1946

After the bombing and destruction of the Grove Road fire station in June, they needed a temporary fire station. The officials arranged to move the fire engines to Southfields Road and offices to Orchard Road.

Bourne Street.   1946 – 1973

The NFS requisitioned land in 1945, and work began in May on the new fire station. Because of the urgent need for new premises, members of the fire service built Bourne Street station. The Mayor, Alderman E. C. Martin, on the 10 May 1946 officially opened Bourne Street fire station. Although the NFS had moved operations from Southfields Road into the building on 18 March.

After the opening ceremony and an inspection of the gathered fireman, the Mayor unveiled a tablet in memory of the Eastbourne firemen that lost their lives during the war. They then served tea in the dining room. Accompanying the Mayor at the ceremonies were representatives from the Council, Police, the Government and Fire Regional Officers. The building contained a dormitory where the watch-duty men could sleep, a large mess room, bathrooms, offices, workshops and a telephone switchboard. There were six bays, and the building had a corrugated roof. At the rear was a 60ft drill and hose drying tower.

April 1991 saw the demolition of the old fire station in a million-pound development for twenty-three new apartments. The building had been derelict for some time since its last tenants, Harris Builders Merchants, and a car workshop vacated.

ESRO

Bourne Street (E/B Gazette 15 August 1964)

Guy Bowes

Whitley Road. 1973 –

Back in early 1899 in Captain Hounsom's report, it mentions that they could build a new fire station in Whitley Road. He said they should sell the Cavendish Place fire station as they needed larger premises. There were details of this in the *Eastbourne Gazette* of 29 March, and for several years' discussions took place with various sites around the town suggested.

So, after many years of discussion, they gave instructions to Mr H. Connolly, the Borough Architect. He was to draw up plans and submit them to the Council. Construction on the one-acre grounds of the new building started in January 1972, and they laid the foundation stone on 20 April 1972.

On the 4 Dec 1973, the Duke of Norfolk, Lord Lieutenant of Sussex accompanied by the Mayor, Sir Sydney Caffyn performed the official opening.

The building constructed by E. Powell & Sons Limited had space for six appliances and had a two-bay workshop. It occupies one acre with a frontage of 234ft to Whitley Road and 201ft to Chawbrook Road. On the ground floor, there are offices, a control room, conference room, mess recreation room and the kitchen. There are also lockers, lecture room and breathing apparatus maintenance room. The upper floor accommodates more offices for the Chief Fire Officer and his Deputy, as well as for typing and clerical staff. There are dormitories/restrooms and a television and study room. On the site, there is also a fifty-foot-high drill and hose drying tower, a two-storey training building, repair shop and extra space for storing equipment. At the rear of the building is a large drill yard, together with five garages for brigade vehicles and car parking space for staff. A diesel-operated generator provides secondary lighting and supplies facilities for the radio and telephone communications in an emergency. The floor space in the new station is 18,683 sq. ft. The cost of construction of the building was £190,000.

****

E/B Gazette 30 April 1952

Practice at Bourne Street.

1954 Bedford Tender + 1951 Dennis F.12   *Brian Jones*

Heritage Eastbourne

Mid 1950s Xmas Party

10 RECREATION

Besides all the drills and waiting around, crews involved themselves with many other activities to keep the men fit and entertained. The brigade would put on displays for the public in places like Devonshire Park, Gildredge Park, or along the seafront. They would also attend competitions held by the South Coast Division of the Volunteer Fire Brigades and the National Fire Brigades Union. Eastbourne held competitions for invited fire crews from around the county. Some of these involved regular trips to other fire stations.

E/B Gazette 13 October 1954

They also held an annual Fireman's Ball to raise funds for their Sick Benefit Fund. These annual gatherings carried on for many years and raised money for good causes and notably for the Fire Brigades' Association Widows' and Orphans' Fund. The Orphans' Fund awarded a shield for the brigade that collected the most money in the year. Eastbourne won this shield frequently. Also, there was a yearly flower and vegetable show when they sent proceeds to the Firemen's Widows' and Orphans' Fund. Other activities were football matches, snooker competitions, quizzes and other games that were with local clubs and other fire brigades.

For the annual fire brigade outing of the Hastings and St. Leonards Volunteer force in June 1890. They invited Captain Towner and two other men from Eastbourne Fire Brigade to join them on their trip to Brussels and Antwerp.

In the group of about sixty-five participants were Captain Harwood of the Carshalton Fire Brigade and local Hasting's councillors and business owners.

Captain Towner in June requested permission from the Eastbourne Council to take the fire engine 'Morrison' to a competition that was being held in Bexhill on the 7 July 1892. He also requested help with his expenses, and the council agreed.

The competition was in the grounds of the Manor House in Bexhill where the Hastings Brigade won first prize. Eastbourne came second and received a cup for their contest in the Manual engine race.

The brigade also supported fellow institutions, as in September 1894, when Eastbourne held the 'Lifeboat Saturday Procession' in aid of funds for the Royal Lifeboat Institution. Eastbourne Fire Brigade under Captain J. Towner attended with three engines, each drawn by four horses. On this occasion the Hailsham Fire Brigade also attended.

Twenty-four members of the Eastbourne brigade attended a dinner party at Cavendish Road Station on the 7th January 1901. They held this in the reception room on the first floor above the fire engines, with Fireman C. Hobden providing the catering. The room was suitably decorated for the New Year, and after dinner, there were speeches, drinks and a sing-a-long.

After WW2, the brigade arranged annual flower shows and set up cricket, football and snooker teams that competed locally.

In August 1948, the Eastbourne fire crews answered a call from the Fire Service National Benevolent Fund. When they agreed to host a group of fifteen orphans for a week's holiday in the town. They were children of firefighters who had lost their parents during the war. All the children, aged between 6½ and 14 years, stayed with Eastbourne firemen and their families during their week's holiday. The arranged to feed the children in the fire station canteen.

Also, in August but this time in 1952, the Mayor, Alderman E. C. Martin presented a trophy to Fireman F. Kirkland. This was the Snooker Cup presented to him for winning the recent competition.

FIREMAN F. KIRKMAN being presented with the Snooker Cup by the Mayor (Ald. E. C. Martin) at the Fire Station. On the right is Chief Officer S. A. Phillips. Report on page 5.

E/B Gazette 20 August 1952

October 1953 and the local brigade sent a team to participate in a quiz night, which was between various brigades for a chance to go to the finals of the fire brigade competition. They held the contest at the Fire Service College, Dorking, and Eastbourne narrowly won the night.

MEMBERS of the five-man Eastbourne Fire Brigade team, which has reached the final of the all-England quiz competition to be held at the Fire Service College, Dorking, on November 21, are seen near an appliance at the local headquarters.

Herald Chronicle 7 November 1953

Some events the Brigade attended.

1871 Competition at Shoreham Gardens near Brighton.

1872 Competition Alexandra Palace, London. First prize in Manual fire engine.

1873 Competition 10 November Crystal Palace, London. Against fifteen other teams, they won first prize for four-man drill.

1877 Competition 2 July Alexandra Palace, London. Won second Steam prize.

1878 Competition 2 September Shoreham. Third prize in fire engine practice.

1879 Tunbridge Wells, Kent. Won challenge cup plus the first prize for Steam and second and third prize for Manual engine work.

1891 Brigade Display. 11 July Crystal Palace.

1892 Competition 7 July Bexhill. First and second prizes in various competitions.

1898 Competition August Blenheim Park. In the Barratt Hose Cart Shield, Eastbourne achieved 3rd prize and diploma for their hose cart team.

1899 Competition 17 May at Devonshire Park. 1st prize for district Steamer winning the new challenge shield. 2nd prize for four-man hose cart, and 3rd prize for district escape competition and half-mile cycle race. The national fireman's competition was held at Perry Bar, Birmingham in July and in the wet drill contest for Steamers, Eastbourne won fourth prize.

1903 Competition 20 May Devonshire Park, Eastbourne. This was for qualifying for the National Fire Brigades' Union contest at Earl's Court, London. Which they held between 9-18 of July. Nine other teams took part, but Eastbourne could only achieve a third place in one event. They came fourth in another and second in the Tug of War.

THE DEVONSHIRE PARK.

NATIONAL FIRE BRIGADES' UNION.

THE ANNUAL

DISTRICT COMPETITIONS

Will be held as above,

THIS DAY (WEDNESDAY), MAY 20th,

Commencing at Two o'clock sharp.

The splendid "Eastbourne" Challenge Shield and Worthing Challenge Cup, will be competed for, also competitions to qualify for the National Events at Earl's Court in July, in Steamers, Manuals, Fire Escapes, Hose Carts, &c. Also a Popular Programme of Sports.

A Band will be in Attendance.

Admission £d. Subscribers Free. Enclosure 6d. Extra.

E/B Gazette 20 May 1903

1904 Competition 29 June Hastings. 2nd prize in the four-man hose-cart drill.

1939 Competition 15 July Hailsham.

1951 Saturday 25 August and the brigade held its second annual flower show in Bourne Street station. The Mayor attended and there were donations to the Fire Service Benevolent Fund.

1964 Competition July Maresfield. Winning AFS cup (Portable Pump Drill) and winning again in 1966 and 1967.

11 EQUIPMENT

1824. First known fire appliance with the Vestry.

1853. July. Shand Mason Manual appliance. This was in 1912 sold to a businessman, renovated and presented to the Pevensey Fire Brigade.

1867. Merryweather Escape ladder.

1871. Merryweather appliance purchased.

1873. Merryweather Steamer engine named the 'Sutton'. Delivering 350 gallons of water per minute with two deliveries.

1876. Merryweather Steam engine purchased. Named the 'Fire King' it belonged to the private brigade stationed in Langney Road. Merryweather had designed this engine and exhibited it at a recent exhibition before they sent it to Eastbourne.

After lighting the fire, it would take nine minutes for the engine to reach 70 to 100lbs per inch of pressure and water could be projected 150 feet.

1890. Steam fire engine. This was a Merryweather horizontal Greenwich pattern model. Which they named 'Morrison'; this engine was still in use in 1927.

Guy Bowes

Picture from 1932 with Fireman Frank Ticehurst holding the reins.

1899. Report listing appliances available. 1 Manual engine, 2 Merryweather Steamers, 3 fire escapes and hose carts with hoses.

1903. Purchase of Merryweather 'Curricle' Escape ladder. A lightweight machine with a reach of 40ft and could travel horizontally and be operated by one man.

(Report 2x 50ft escape ladders, 2x Merryweather Steam engines).

1911. July. Merryweather "Greenwich" pattern 40ft telescopic fire escape ladder includes a box for 60ft hose and other gear.

Robert Sumsion

Departing Grove Road

1912. September. Eastbourne's first motor engine was ordered in March and delivered in September. It was a Leyland Motor Pump and Escape Appliance, model U.55V costing £925.

The registration number was HC 235. This vehicle came with solid tyres, acetylene gas headlights and a 4 cylinder 58 hp engine that drove a water pump with a capacity of 400 /500 gallons a minute, and capable of raising a jet of water 150 feet. It also carried a 50ft wheeled Fire Escape (later a 65ft escape) and a First Aid Hose Reel Apparatus from a 50-gallon tank. The unit had an 8-inch suction hose mounted on solid tyres.

They put the engine into reserve in 1932. Later in June 1933, Eastbourne sold it to Haywards Heath Fire Brigade.

1916. Report states brigade has one motor fire engines, two steamers, six fire escapes, five hose carts and reels and five fire stations.

Michael Garrett

1924** July. Dennis Braidwood Motor Pump and Escape, with registration number HC 4273 and costing £1,622. With a 50/60 hp motor turbine engine with a self-starter and electric lighting. It had a 50ft Bayleys wheeled fire escape, 400/500 g.p.m centrifugal pump and first aid hose reel apparatus. The Dennis could only draw water from one hydrant. In 1931 they fitted pneumatic tyres, the following year they converted it to a fast motor pump and the 50ft ladder replaced with a 35ft extending ladder. 1939 they restored to its original setup with a 50ft ladder and known as the Dennis Stand-By Combination. The engine was sold in 1951 for £75.

1932** May. Merryweather (Dorman). 100ft Turntable four-section Ladder with a 6 cylinder 90 hp engine, fitted with steel disc wheels with servo-operated brakes and solid India rubber tyres. The rear wheels have twin tyres. Registration number JK 2329. This cost £2,975 and had a 60-gallon First Aid Hose Reel apparatus and searchlight. Also provided was hydraulic pattern hose reel with 180ft of rubber hose. A monitor jet was fitted to the top of the ladders. In 1937 they fitted pneumatic tyres and in 1939 a two-way telephone so there was contact between the top of the ladders and the ground controller.

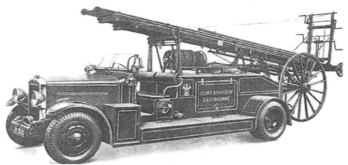

1932. Morris** Commercial Braidwood design Escape Van, registration number JK 2330, with a windscreen and a 70 hp, six-cylinder engine. This appliance had cost £975. It had a 60-gallon hose reel tank and the reel operated by a five-way valve and two hook ladders, 1,000ft of hose in 100ft lengths. It had a 50ft wooden wheeled Baileys Escape Ladder. This was from the 1912 Leyland appliance. There was a locker that went right through the appliance, which meant they could run a hose run out from either side of the vehicle. This appliance became the second pump in 1936 and later sold in 1954.

Roger Mardon

1936** January. Dennis Limousine FS6 Enclosed Pump covered fire engine. Chassis number 7740. Registration number JK 5040 used as an Emergency Tender with a crew of ten. The Dennis company constructed this vehicle to Chief Fire Officer Spence's specifications. It had a six-cylinder engine developing 110 bhp and a mid-mounted 650/800 g.p.m pump, 40-gallon First Aid Hose Reel tank. Carrying a

Robert Sumsion

35ft Ajax telescopic ladder, two hook ladders, four scaling ladders and 2,000ft of hose. There was a canteen kit with Primus stove and kettle for the six men, driver and officer crew.

Other equipment supplied was a hydraulic and other lifting jack, one 5 ton and a 20 ton for heavy lifts, and oxy-acetylene cutting equipment. Also, 2 x 1-hour Proto BA sets, with CO2 and oxygen. It also had twin 12-volt batteries, a 3½ kw 110-volt dynamo, flood and searchlights. The headlamps were detachable and crews could place them on tripods for illumination at the scene of the incident. The engine cost £2,225. It was out of service 1958.

Ford Prefect

** The government returned these machines to Eastbourne when the County Borough Council regained control over the fire service in April 1948.

The Council also took over appliances acquired by the AFS in 1946.

1940/1. Dennis Trailer Pumps 350/500 g.p.m (2).

1941/3. Beresford Stork Trailer Pumps 120 g.p.m (2).

The 1940s. Austin Towing Vehicle. (2) 1942 Registration number GLE 238, used as a service van and painted green. The second Registration number GXH 135. Both were built on the Austin K2 2-ton chassis with a six-cylinder 3.46 litre 60 bhp petrol engine.

1943. Austin Salvage Tender. They later fitted it with a First Aid Hose Reel pump, a portable pump and salvage and other equipment taken from the 1935 Dennis Limousine. Out of service by 1958, and replaced in 1961 by the Morris Utility Tender.

1943. Dodge Kew Water Tender, 3-4 ton with six stud wheels and a 450-gallon water tank. Registration Number GXM 624. This was modernised from an MDU to WRT'A' in the early 1950s and fitted with a new

Michael Garrett

body, model 82, a low load 400-gallon water tank. Also, a First Aid Pump and Hose Reel apparatus with a 500gmp pump. Replaced in 1966 by a Bedford Type "B" Water Tender.

David Holt

Later equipment.

Michael Garrett

1951 June. Ordered by the Ministry of Works (WPO 40229/30) and delivered in June a Dennis F12 150-in wheelbase. Chassis number 3482 with registration number AJK 200. A dual-purpose escape appliance with an 8-cylinder Rolls Royce B80 petrol engine. Had a 900/ 1000 g.p.m with No 3 Dennis pump, 400-gallon tank, First Aid Hose Reel Appliance with a 50ft wheeled Escape ladder. Also, a V.H.F. radio, a searchlight and two bells.

One operated by hand and the other electrically from a switch at the feet of the officer in charge. They replaced the Escape ladder in 1949 with a 46ft lightweight alloy extension ladder. Originally the F12 cost £3,750 and was replaced in 1972. They retired this engine in 1975, and it is still in existence and has been restored.

David Holt

1954. Bedford S chassis. Built by HCB-Angus Ltd, body serial number s0161. SLZ Water Tender Type B with Dennis No 2, 250/500 g.m.p pump and an FWP LPP. It carried a 35ft Ajax Extension Ladder and had a 400-gallons water tank. Registration number CHC 800 and supplied by Mansfields of Cornfield Road. In service in February 1955. The cost of this engine with some extras was £2,890. The vehicle was out of service by 1974.

Michael Garrett

Michael Garrett

1955. Dennis (1940) MW 30 100 TLP Sulzer pump. Transferred from London Lambeth to Eastbourne in 1955. Registration number GGK 945. Out of service 1967.

Michael Garrett

1956. Hillman Husky utility van registration number EHC 100 with two-way V.H.F. radio and breathing equipment. Car and equipment cost £775.

1961. Walker & Evans built on a Morris 30 cwt chassis; a Forward Control known as a Morris Utility Emergency Tender. Registration number JJK 200. that cost £4,000. They replaced the Morris in 1966 when they bought a new Bedford HCB-Angus with ET body.

1961 Austin Mini. Registration number JJK 100.

1965. Bedford Diesel built on a KH chassis, by HCB-Angus, standard WrT, body serial number s1313, registration number CJK 888D. With a 30-foot extension ladder, 400-gallons tank, and an HCB-Angus 500 g.p.m pump, FWPS LPP. Records show the cost

Aidan Fisher

of the appliance was £4,000. They replaced the 30ft extension ladder in 1969 with similar 46ft alloy extending ladder.

Michael Garrett

The Ian Moore Collection

1966. Bedford built on a KH chassis by HCB-Angus with ET body, Body serial number s1473, It carried a 35ft Ajax ladder and 130 gallons of water with HCB 250/500 g.p.m. pump. It also had oxy-acetylene and propane cutting equipment, breathing apparatus, an Emergency Electricity Generator together with flood and searchlights. Registration number DJK 999F. The cost of this engine was £5,572.

Jerry Hepworth

1967. January. Merryweather built on an AEC Mercury chassis with the registration number DHC 222E. It carried a 100ft steel turntable ladder and had a 300 g.p.m pump. This engine cost £12,205, and the brigade sold this machine in 1990 for £1,285 as they were having problems getting spares. It was replaced by a new 1987

ESRO

Angloco MAN/Metz DLK 30. Registration number E 184 BPN. This vehicle was still in service in 1994.

Simon Ryan

Ex AFS 1968 (1954) Land Rover 88 S1. Canvasback and fitted with a large roof rack and used to tow a two-wheeled trailer. Cliff Rescue Unit. Registration number LYO 837. Personnel Carrier Land Rover ex HOFSTS as part of Mobile Fire Column Fire Company Section, Convoy No 27 to Eastbourne. Ex AFS 1968.

1969. Ford Escort van registration number GHC 216G.

1970. Bedford built on a KH chassis with HCB-Angus PHP bodywork, body serial no. 2057. Registration number GJK 600H. It had a Simon SS50 PHP hydraulic platform, and 2 x 125-gallon water tanks with 500 g.p.m. HCB pump. The cost of this appliance was £10,000 and it was out of service in 1988.

Aidan Fisher

1972. Ford D1014 chassis with Carmichael D Water Tender. With 400-gallon water tank and 500 g.p.m pump, First Aid Hose Reel. Plus, a 46ft Alloy Extending ladder.

Shaun Rogers

Registration number MHC 750L. This cost £8,400.

They transferred the tender to Rye Fire Brigade in the late 1970s as this was one of the few appliances that would fit into the low ceiling bays in Rye station house. It was used up to 1989 and disposed of around 1990.

1973. The fire appliances in town when the new fire station was opened in December 1973 were:

1966 Bedford Water Tender Ladder. CJK 888D. (1)

1967 AEC Merryweather 100ft Turntable Ladder. DHC 222E. (3)

1966 Bedford Pump/Emergency Salvage Tender. DJK 999F. (2)

1969/1970 Bedford 50ft Hydraulic Platform and Pump. GJK 600H. (4)

1969. Ford Escort Cliff RT van, registration number GHC 216.

1972 Ford Water Tender Ladder. MHC 750L. (5)

****

Whitley Road   *ESRO*

E/B Gazette 23 March 1963   *ESRO*

*Michael
Garrett*

12 CHIEF OFFICERS

Manual	Section	Steam	Section
William Simpson	11.1853-1867	-	-
Charles Tomes	8.1867-4.1871	-	-
Henry Brown	5.1871-12.1873	Thomas Fuller	1873-1884
James Towner	12.1873-1896	Gausden	1884-1896

Years			Rank	FirstName	Surname
1897	1931	E/B	Captain	John	Hounsom
.6.1931	2.5.1938	Boro	Chief Officer	Douglas W.	Spence
6.8.1938	.8.1941	Fire	Chief Officer	Sydney A.	Philips
1941 until	1948		National	Fire	Service
.8.1948	30.6.1953	Boro	Chief Officer	Sydney A.	Phillips
3.9.1953	14.1.1955	E/B	Chief Officer	Charles J.	Murrant
23.1.1956	31.12.1964	Brig	Chief Officer	Pat Charles	Short
1.1.1965	31.10.1968	"	Chief Officer	W. F.	Dancey
1.11.1968	31.3.1974	"	Chief Officer	Frank P.	Tarling

****

January 1970 E/B Pier Theatre Fire   *ESRO*

June 1933   Royal Marine Laundry Fire   *ESRO*

13 SOME MAJOR INCIDENTS

Date	Month	Year	Place
17	November	1874	Peerless Timber Yard, Langney Road.
11	June	1878	Golden Hop Brewery, E/B.
20	December	1891	Ratton Hall, Willingdon.
12	January	1896	Peerless Timber Yard, Langney Road.
12	August	1899	Farm at Willingdon.
29	September	1927	All Saints' Church, Carlisle Road.
08	June	1933	Royal Marine Laundry, Winchelsea Rd.
(07	February	1943	Grove Rd Brigade headquarters bombed).
23	January	1958	South Street.
25	August	1958	Glasgow-Eastbourne Car sleeper train crash at Rail station.
06	April	1966	Fire at Beachy Head Hotel, Beachy Head.
20	October	1968	Explosion and fire on board SS *"Sitakund"*.
08	January	1970	Fire on Eastbourne pier. Pier theatre.

Peerless Timber Yard. 17 November 1874.

Fire destroyed the business and work yards of Messrs James Peerless, a local builder. The premises were at the corner of Langney Road and Terminus Road and comprised offices, wheelwrights' shop, and carpenters' workrooms. With a paint shop and stables nearby. They estimated the damage to the property to be £4,000 to £5,000. The two engines from the Volunteer Fire Brigade attended with help from the army appliances. The old Manual fire engine from Compton Place was also in attendance. Army crews came from the Redoubt, and the Royal Engineers stationed at Langney assisted the firefighters.

Coastguard crews also helped the firemen by directing hoses into the fire. Fire crews arrived at 10.15 p.m. and evacuated the surrounding buildings. This was a difficult fire for them to attack as public houses, a brewery, a hotel and private residences surrounded the premises. At about 1 a.m., a boiler in the yard burst, destroying a brick wall by Langney Road.

It was not until 3 a.m. the following morning that the fire was under control. The fire crews were in attendance all day, damping down small fires. The inferno destroyed the carpenter's shop, painter's shop, stables and offices. The roofs at the malt-house and the Lion Brewery sustained substantial damage. No lives were lost, and they saved four horses, but the blaze badly damaged some brigade equipment.

Golden Hop Brewery. 07 June 1878.

Late in the evening, about 1 a.m. on Friday, a patrolling police officer discovered the fire when he noticed smoke coming from the boiler room of the Golden Hop Brewery, Seaside Road. Mr Edward Hollingham, who lived nearby, owned the brewery and dispatched someone to the nearby fire station in Langney Road. But there was a delay with problems raising any assistance. At last, the watchman despatched a hose to the fire whilst waiting for more firemen to attend. Unfortunately, while trying to attach the hose, they found a branch pipe was missing. The day before, the firemen cleaned and overhauled the engine, and they mislaid the branch pipe.

By the time they brought the branch pipe to the scene, the whole building was alight. There was now the added danger of exploding beer barrels. The Army barracks engine supported the firemen. But they and the town engine could not save the building, which the fire gutted. The Army engine from the barracks was first on the scene. Followed closely by the Eastbourne Fire Brigade's Steam engine, and then the Manual engine.

By the time the Steam engine got fired up, the whole brewery was alight. A brewery worker had a lucky escape when at ten minutes to two, the brewery roof collapsed.

The coastguard assisted by forming a line around the firemen to keep onlookers away and safe. They estimated the damage sustained to be more than £3,000, but Mr Hollingham had insured the building.

At this time, there was no alarm bell attached to the firehouse, and the firemen all lived in different parts of the town. This delayed their actions in putting out the fire. The blaze destroyed the brewery, a substantial square-built four-storey brick structure. But firefighters were praised for their efforts in saving adjoining buildings.

Ratton Hall. 20 December 1891.

Staff at Ratton Hall, Willingdon, owned by Mr Freeman Thomas J.P. (who was away at the time) noticed smoke coming from the house early on Sunday morning. This was a devastating fire that destroyed the building. They discovered the fire at 5.30 a.m., and speedily despatched messengers to Hailsham and Eastbourne, asking for urgent help. The fire had started in the upper storeys of the forty roomed Manor House and had quickly spread through the entire building.

They reported in the *Eastbourne Gazette* that the firemen could see the blaze reflected in the sky from Eastbourne. Both the 'Morrison' and 'Sutton' from Cavendish Place under the command of Engineer Perry, together with the Manual engine with Engineer J. Newman from Old Town, attended. When the firefighters arrived at about 7 a.m., the roof was ablaze and soon collapsed, and there were little the firemen could do.

Twenty-seven firefighters attended but could not save the premises even though the water supply was sufficient, as there were two hydrants close by. One was at the rear and one at the property's front. They positioned the 'Morrison' at the side of the house and then attached two separate lengths of hose to each engine. The outside walls, entrance hall, and two or three rooms survived the blaze. They estimated the damage to the house at about £4,000, plus £1,000 for the furniture. The family had insured the house and contents with the Sun Fire Office.

Peerless Timber Yard. 12 January 1896.

Early Sunday morning on the 12th saw one of the largest fires that Eastbourne had seen for many years. Mr Stephen Daw noticed a fire coming from the workshops and hastened to the fire station in Cavendish Place. He reported that the building yard full of stocks of wood, that faced Langney Road, was ablaze and the roof of the workshops was nearly off. The premises belonged to Messrs James Peerless.

Déjà vu, as there had been a very large fire at the yard back in 1874 which many of the current firemen had attended. The two-storied building and yard were situated with the Lion Brewery at the rear and close by the Carpenters' Arms and Diplock's Commercial Hotel.

Fronting the yard were eight sections, each fourteen feet long, with the engine house some sixty-feet-long, with a fifty feet high shaft. The workshop constructed with yellow brick stood three storeys high and was about 150ft long. Lost in the fire were stables, a horse, a pony and a four-wheeled spring van and dogcart. Two firemen trying to rescue the horses narrowly escaped injury when the roof of the stables gave way. Slates from the roof fell on Fireman S. Gausden (son of the Superintendent), denting his helmet, and Fireman Denton just managed to escape before the roof of the stables collapsed.

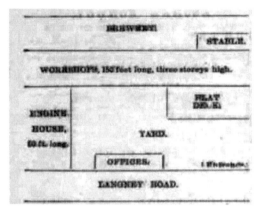

E/B Gazette 15 January 1896

Timber and furniture were lost together with the paint store, but the brigade saved the engine and engine house. The estimate for damage caused that day was £4,000.

Eastbourne's fire engines 'Morrison' and 'Sutton' with the fire escape ladder attended the fire together with men from the Old Town fire station. Twenty-eight firemen were in attendance under the command of Superintendents Hounsom and Gausden. At one time eight jets of water from various points were being directed onto the fire, but they could not save the builder's yard. In just over two hours they brought the fire under control, and the firemen concentrated their effort on saving the nearby properties.

After the earlier fire at the yard, the company had built an eighteen-inch party wall. This was between the Peerless property and the brewery. That helped to save further damage to the adjoining business.

The Steamers worked from Langney and Terminus Roads. Whilst the Manual appliance fought the fire from the corner of Pevensey Road. The firemen were at the scene until after mid-day Sunday damping down the embers. It would take three months to rebuild the

E/B Gazette 15 January 1896

business, and many men would be out of work until they constructed the new buildings.

Park Farm. 12 August 1899.

On Saturday night, about eleven o'clock, a dreadful fire occurred at Mr William Carter's Park Farm in Willingdon. Farmworkers discovered the fire in a large barn full of farm implements and sacks of wheat, oats, rye, and wool. Mr Carter and his farmhands had only just finished harvesting that afternoon.

He sent messengers to inform the Willingdon Fire Brigade. They were under the command of Engineer Russell and rushed to the scene. The farm employees also telephoned the Eastbourne police. They contacted the Eastbourne Fire Brigade, and Captain J.A. Hounsom was soon on the scene with the 'Morrison' and 'Sutton' engines, but they could not save the barn. The crews (thirty men in total) set about trying to save the nearby house and other outbuildings. It was not until early the following morning at about 1 a.m. that they brought the fire under control. The Eastbourne Fire Brigade returned to their stations, except for a dozen men under the command of Superintendent Perry left to help with the remnants of the fire. It took until Sunday evening for them to completely extinguished the fire. The estimated damage was about £1,500. The Cavendish Place Fire Station received the call about the fire at 10.55 p.m. They had wanted to leave at once. But as the fire was in Willingdon and outside of their area, they had to wait for authority to attend. This meant that there was a delay, and the firefighters finally departed for Willingdon at 11.55 p.m.

All Saints' Church. 29 September 1927.

On the evening of Thursday 29th, about 5.40 the brigade received a call about a fire in the All Saints' Church in Carlisle Road. Within minutes the first engine with Engineer Eldridge in charge left, shortly followed by a second. Crews (about thirty men) were despatch from Grove Road, Cavendish Place, Meads and Old Town. They did not need help from the Hampden Park fire station. The first firefighters arrived on scene within 4½ minutes. The pitch-pine church roof was well alight when the men arrived and soon collapsed. Crews concentrated their efforts on saving the Vestry and tower and stopping the fire from spreading to nearby adjoining houses. It was an awful night with the rain pouring down and a westerly wind blowing furiously.

The brigade had seven deliveries from hydrants and two from their pump playing on the fire and used forty lengths of 60ft hose. The hydrants used were from Wish Road, Carlisle Road, and Grange Road and supplied ample pressure – about 125 lbs. One fire engine returned to their station at 8 p.m. as it was not needed.

The other returned at 9.30 p.m. Six firefighters and a turncock stayed on duty all night. Captain Hounsom was not on scene as he was away from Eastbourne on business. He had departed that morning to attend the Fire Brigades' Autumn Conference in Leeds.

Royal Marine Laundry. 08 June 1933.

On Thursday morning 8 June, just after six o'clock, a passer-by discovered a fire at the Royal Marine Laundry in Winchelsea Road. Flames were seen rising to a height of sixty feet from the building. It was six thirty-five when the police informed the fire brigade, and the motor escape with Chief Officer Spence, 2nd Officer Phillips and four men immediately departed. Three minutes later, three auxiliary firemen followed with the motor ladders. A few minutes later, another five firemen and the motor pump joined them. The escape was quickly hooked up to three hydrants. They used two other hydrants in Vine Square, and the Dennis motor pump started ten deliveries from the cutting leading to the nearby yachting pond.

The firemen surrounded the building and had the blaze under control by nine a.m. and a 'Stop' command was issued. There had been a danger from falling roofs and walls, but there were not any casualties reported.

Although when a gas meter exploded, it caused some concern. The fire destroyed the main building, built of brick, timber and corrugated iron. The buildings involved in the fire covered an area of about 200ft by 60ft. As the business was in a residential part of town, hundreds of spectators turned out to watch the firefighters at work and watched the flames rising to a height of sixty feet from the buildings. Police were present and controlled the crowds.

Although they lost the main building, the brigade stopped the fire from reaching the boiler room and an explosion of the boilers. They estimated the damage to be thousands of pounds.

E/B Gazette 10 June 1933

Marine Laundry

F. R. Pinker Ltd. 23 January 1958.

Shortly after 5.00 a.m. on Thursday, Mr E. Pounds discovered a fire at 2a South Street. The premises of the wholesale company of F.R. Pinker Ltd. He immediately ran across the road to the police station. Once notified by the police, the fire engines departed to the fire. The fire was in buildings behind the New Hotel and on arrival, the crews found that the flames were visible thirty feet above the building. Station Officer R. Scarlett was in charge with a pump escape, and the water tender. He also had the 100ft turntable ladder and emergency tender.

Five hose lines used hydrants in Furness Road and South Street, and the firefighters brought the fire under control within an hour. Firemen remained on the scene during Thursday, damping down the embers.

There were not any casualties except for Fireman Wooller, who sustained a cut thumb when a falling slate hit him. They treated him at the scene. The *Eastbourne Herald Chronicle* reported that this was the worst fire since the end of the war and South Street was closed for three hours. The building was gutted, and the blaze destroyed stock, two lorries and several pianos. They estimated the damage sustained at £13,000.

Eastbourne station train crash. 25 August 1958.

The worst tragedy to happen in Eastbourne in peacetime happened early on Monday morning, just as the 7.25 electric commuter train was about to depart from the station. The train was running seven minutes late and waiting to depart when the incoming Glasgow Car-Sleeper steam train struck it head-on. Almost immediately the police, the fire service under the command of Chief Fire Officer Mr P. C. Short, and St John Ambulance Brigade went to the aid of the passengers. The railway station staff joined them. The impact hurled the first two carriages from the electric train into the air. They hit an overhead gantry and landed on the Glasgow train, and the collision forced the rear of the Eastbourne train into the platform buffers.

```
                    --------------------
                      EMERGENCY SERVICES.

Eastbourne Police were called at ..............................7.31am
One Policeman was in attendance at ...........................7.31am
Several more arrived at ......................................7.32/33am
Three Doctors were called by Eastbourne Police at ............7.35am
One had arrived by ...........................................7.38am
The other two were in attendance by ..........................7.40am
Ambulance service was called by Eastbourne Police at .........7.31/32am
One ambulance was on site at .................................7.33am
Followed shortly afterwards by 4 more also 3 dual purpose
          vehicles and 2 cars.
Eastbourne Fire Brigade were called by means of radio by
                Eastbourne Police at .........................7.57am
Fire Brigade arrived on site at ..............................7.58am
St. Marys Hospital advised by Eastbourne Police at ...........7.31am
Princess Alice Hospital advised by Eastbourne Police at ......7.31am
G.P.O. informed by Eastbourne Police at ......................7.40am
W.V.S.    "      "      "     "     "    ......................8.35am

   The Eastbourne County Borough Transport Department made available
their oxy-acetylene cutting plant and breakdown vehicle, equipped with
tools and jacks, for use in freeing trapped passengers.
```

Report on emergency services.

This had been the 6.47 Ore to London Bridge service, a regular commuter service. It was usually a six-coach service, but on this day, it had twelve coaches. Because of this, passengers were spread throughout the train. There was only one passenger in the first carriage of the electric train and just a few in the second, otherwise, there could have been even more casualties. In total five people, four men (one being the driver) and one woman, all on the electric train lost their lives with forty-one other passengers injured. There was only one casualty on the steam train with minor injuries with the train driver and fireman suffering from shock. The 57-year-old driver of the electric train was not so lucky.

The Glasgow train had departed at 7.47 p.m. with thirty-six passengers and eleven cars. Two of the Glasgow's train carriages telescoped together, but fortunately, these were the car carriages. One of the these was a car carriage and was sliced in two.

Beachy Head Hotel. 06 April 1966.

The single-storey Beachy Head Hotel had recently received a £60,000 face-lift when early Wednesday morning a disastrous fire broke out. The brigade with three fire engines had problems with a water supply and with the strong winds could not save the hotel. Because of the shortage of water, the brigade had to ferry up supplies at 400 gallons each trip. They reported at the time that flames leapt 50ft into the air.

Herald Chronicle 9 April 1966

Thankfully, although a devastating fire, there were not any casualties. After dampening down, all that remained of the hotel were the chimney stacks and the fireplace in the restaurant.

"*Sitakund*" tanker. 20 October 1968.

After discharging her cargo of oil in Wilhelmshaven, the *Sitakund*, a Norwegian tanker set off for Libya. Whilst she was about seventeen miles off the coast at Holywell, there were two enormous explosions. The ship's hull was breached, and fire broke out. This happened at 20.00 hours, and the fire spread to the engine room, stores and crew's quarters. The first explosion took place in the starboard tanks, with a further explosion in the after centre and port tanks below the waterline. Now there was danger of further explosions, as the detonations had not affected her cargo tanks, which contained an explosive mixture of oil vapour and air.

A group of French trawlers were first on the scene and rescued thirty-one members of the crew that had launched lifeboats and rowed towards them. The captain and six of his men stayed on board to extinguish the flames even though there was still a threat of further explosions.

The Eastbourne and Newhaven lifeboats were both launched to give help and to look for missing crewmen.

The frigate H.M.S. *Mohawk*, sailing from Portsmouth to Rosyth, Fife, received orders to assist the damaged tanker. It took on board the rescued crews from the French trawlers and transported them to the Royal Naval hospital in Haslar, Gosport. They reported that three crew members had died in the explosion.

They sent the British Railways tug *Meeching* moored in Newhaven out to the

stricken vessel to aid in the fire and recovery. Their crew got a man and a line aboard and then towed the stricken tanker to Eastbourne Bay. They also sent the Dover based tug *Dominant* to help. And they and the *Meeching* managed to ground the *Sitakund* on

E/B Gazette 23 October 1968

rocks a little west of Dukes Mound.

Eastbourne's firemen were called to assist and requested extra foam from the East Sussex Brigade. A fire crew of ten men with their Chief and Deputy Fire Officers used the pier as a staging point to assemble two fire monitors and eight jets. With the help of *Irene*, a local fishing boat equipped with two-way radio, they travelled out to the still blazing ship. The *Dominant* and the *Meeching* crew with monitors mounted on top of their wheelhouses and the eight jets successfully put the fire out. The fire in the tanker's side was subdued by mid-afternoon. There were still fires burning in the stern and accommodation section of the vessel, and

they positioned four jets to attack this area.

On Tuesday afternoon, they retrieved two bodies.

In the early hours of Wednesday, Chief Fire Officer Dancey requested an extra 200

Jets from a tug attack the fire from the stern

Photo: Daily Mail

gallons of foam, 30 lengths of hose and two mechanical generators.

The lifeboat *Beryl Tolllemarche* ferried the supplies of equipment with BA appliances out to the firefighters. Later in the day, Hailsham Fire Brigade sent a crew out to the blazing ship to relieve Eastbourne crews, whilst a team from Pevensey Fire Brigade were on standby. It was not until Friday afternoon at 13.33 that the Eastbourne and East Sussex fire crews received a 'Stop' message, and the weary crews could stand down.

It was suggested that the *Sitakund* crew had not properly vented the cargo tanks of flammable gases. And this was most likely the reason for the accident. Whilst the Eastbourne Brigade were fighting the fire, East Sussex Fire Service provided cover for the town.

Team involved with *Sitakund* incident   *Avril King*

Eastbourne pier. 08 January 1970.

About 2.00 p.m. on Thursday, two staff members working in the auditorium discovered a fire in the Pavilion Theatre. Two GPO engineers, Mr Ernest Smith and Mr M. D. Ward were laying telephone cables on the pier when they noticed smoke billowing from the theatre roof. Mr Smith immediately raised the alarm by smashing the glass and pulling the handle in a nearby fire alarm box. They then got two of the pier's fire hoses and their ladders and fought the fire themselves.

When the fire service received the call about the fire on the 300 metres Eastbourne pier they responded immediately. The first engines were on scene within three minutes. On-shore winds were fanning the blaze, and within fifteen minutes of the firefighters arriving, the ceiling above the stage collapsed. It soon became clear to Chief Fire Officer Tarling that he required more appliances.

He sent a message to local brigades for assistance. Crews from Bexhill, Burwash, Hailsham, Herstmonceux, Lewes and Pevensey attended. Seaford Fire Brigade stood on standby.

At 2.40 p.m., the left hand of the two pagoda towers of the theatre at the shore side collapsed. Its partner tower followed shortly afterwards. They then closed the pier to the public. By this time, sizable crowds of shoppers and residents gathered along the seafront to watch and they had to bring in the police to control the crowds. They soon dispersed when at 3.30 p.m., there was a shower of hailstones followed by snow blown across the pier by the strong winds. The area of seafront road was a maze of hoses with hydrants along the promenade, and outside the Queens Hotel being used. There were six lines of fire hoses stretching along the pier, which they had attached to the fire appliances at the pier entrance. By 4.40 p.m., the firemen had the blaze under control.

When a reporter interviewed Chief Fire Officer Tarling, he said that "fortunately the safety curtain was down when the fire broke out", "that saved the rest

ESRO

of the building". At its height, sixty firefighters, some wearing breathing equipment tackled the blaze. Sussex Police, St John Ambulance service and SEGAS assisted them. The fire with the help of strong on-shore winds gutted the main stage and the dressing room area. It destroyed the wardrobe and theatrical stores. Also destroyed was the old clock and the stairs leading to the camera obscura. Active firefighting operations went on until 10.00 p.m. on Thursday with two members of Eastbourne Fire Brigade on watch duty through the night.

Deputy Chief Fire Officer A. Green and two station officers, Mr L. Fuller and Mr H. Nunn, assisted Mr Tarling, who was in control of operations. There was only one casualty at the fire, Mr Griffin, the assistant pier master, who suffered from smoke inhalation. The St John Ambulance service took him to hospital, but he soon returned to the pier to help fight the fire. A few days later the police arrested an employee of the pier company for arson.

****

14. LAST WORD

Eastbourne should be very proud of its fire service. From the early days, the senior officers in the service did their best to train and equip their men. They supplied them with the best and most up-to-date equipment. Captain Hounsom, especially, should be credited for all his efforts. First, for setting up the Welfare Fund for injured firemen. And later for organising a committee who arranged the Annual Fireman's Ball. This raised funds for the Welfare Fund and National Fire Brigade Charities. He served the town for 53 years and was captain of the brigade for 34 of those years. As captain of the Eastbourne Fire Brigade, he was strongly involved with the Fireman's Trade Union (1918), later to become the Fire Brigade Union (1930) and the local South Coast District organisation. He served as a life governor of the national Widows' and Orphans' Fund.

This early service relied on volunteer men being paid a few shillings to leave work and risk their lives to save people and property until a more organised service came into force. Later men received a salary and taught how fires behave. Then came a move to a more professional and full-time service which started to employ women. First, as telephone operators and Watch room staff, until today where there are women firefighters. Times have changed, and at the time of writing this book, the Chief Fire Officer of the East Sussex Fire & Rescue Service is a talented and well-respected woman, Dawn Whitaker.

The Chief Fire Officers that followed Captain Hounsom brought the service up to date and helped their men to advance their careers. And attend the new fire brigade colleges. With the advancement of knowledge in firefighting, a more professional service appeared.

Days have changed from the hand carts of old, then horse-pulled steam engines and now motor appliances carrying large turntable ladders. The service has modernised, and the personnel of Eastbourne are now better trained and have a better understanding of how fires behave.

The service, of course, has not only had to deal with conventional fires but receives many other calls for assistance. Whether this is a chimney fire (not so much these days), people locked out of or trapped in their homes, car accidents and fuel spill or the occasional cat stuck up a tree.

These are some of the many incidents they have to attend to, but false alarms are still a problem for the modern service. The service has for many years offered advice on fire management to private business, schools and hotels, together with guidance to householders on fire protection.

After the Fire Services Act 1947, the government disbanded the National Fire Service. Firefighting then returned to the responsibility of county and county borough councils. Brighton, Hastings and Eastbourne managed their own brigades. The government reformed the Auxiliary Fire Service in 1948 to work alongside the Civil Defence Corps and fire service, but they both were disbanded in 1968. In the mid-1970s, they reorganised the local government and amalgamated the borough brigades of Brighton & Hove, Hastings and Eastbourne into the East Sussex Fire Brigade. Between about 1992 and 1997, the service name changed to the East Sussex County Fire Brigade. Then again, there was change when on 1st April 1997, the service came under the newly created East Sussex Fire Authority. The Brigade name changed back to the East Sussex Fire Brigade. With the passing of the Fire and Rescue Service Act 2004, the service changed its name again to the East Sussex Fire & Rescue Service, with 24 fire stations under its control.

I hope this short book proves of interest and illuminates an important piece of Eastbourne's history.

****

1958 Sleeper Train Crash

15 BIBLIOGRAPHY

Aspden, J.C – *Municipal History of Eastbourne 1938-1971* – 1977 – Eastbourne Borough Council.

Chambers, George. F – *Eastbourne Memories* – 1910 – V.T. Sumfield, Station Street.

Fovargue, H.W – *Municipal Eastbourne 1933-1939* – 1939

Hodges, Gilbert – *Eastbourne's Motor Fire Appliances* – 1975 – Eastbourne Local Historian.

Statham, H. H – *The Builder v89 p459*– 1905 – The Strand, London

Surtees, John – *Eastbourne, A History* – 2002 – Phillimore & Co, Chichester.

Young, Bill – *Make Pumps Ten* – 1994

Young, F. T. Charles – *Fires, Fire engines and Fire Brigades* – 1866 – Lockwood & Co. London.

Street Directories. – Various dates – Gowlands, Picks Blue Book and Kelly's.

Newspapers:
Horsham, West Sussex Journal, Eastbourne Chronicle, Herald and Gazette, Illustrated London News, Daily Mail.

KSH History Forum. South-East History Boards.

****

20 October 1968

E/B Gazette 13 Sept 1967   *ESRO*

FIRE, September, 1971

Operational Statistics 1969-70

Local Authority (1)	Population (2)	Density of Population per acre (3)	No. of separate Fire Stations (4)	Number of calls Received				Appliances and Vehicles—Actual Strength at 31st Dec., 1969								Personnel at 31st Dec., 1969				
				Fires (5)	Chimney Fires (6)	Grass and Heath Fires (7)	Special Services (8)	Pumping Appliances (9)	Water Tenders (10)	Turntable Ladders and Snorkels (11)	Trailer or Portable Pumps (12)	Escape and Extension Ladders (13)	Other special Appliances (14)	Ancillary Vehicles (15)	Whole-time		Part-time		
															Authorised (16)	Actually Serving (17)	Authorised (18)	Actually Serving (19)	
COUNTY BOROUGHS																			
1 Great Yarmouth	50,760	13·79	2	198	122	21	106	1	4	1	8	2	—	5	51	51	24	14	1
2 Burton upon Trent†	50,850	12·04	1	150	126	38	86	1	3	1	2	—	3	3	48	48	20	13	2
3 Dewsbury†	51,560	7·67	1	237	101	62	169	2	2	1	5	—	1	4	58	56	36	33	3
4 Merthyr Tydfil†	56,360	3·18	3	161	116	65	110	1	5	—	—	1	1	5	37	39	36	33	4
5 Wakefield	59,630	10·28	1	148	47	49	90	1	1	1	5	—	1	1	56	57	—	—	5
6 Chester†	60,880	13·07	1	366	105	54	571	5	—	1	4	—	1	2	47	47	20	10	6
7 Barrow in Furness	63,460	5·77	1	307	160	106	234	2	1	1	5	5	2	3	51	50	12	—	7
8 Bury†	67,070	9·02	1	540	90	184	208	2	2	1	5	—	1	3	57	57	—	—	8
9 Hastings†	69,020	9·03	2	182	91	79	243	2	3	1	6	9	1	5	49	49	32	12	9
10 Eastbourne†	69,290	6·10	1	187	125	19	406	—	2	1	—	—	3	4	51	51	16	8	10
11 Warrington†	70,870	15·28	1	420	20	127	111	—	4	1	2	1	2	3	80	73	12	1	11
12 Carlisle*	71,090	11·67	1	264	66	63	250	3	1	1	5	6	1	5	56	58	20	2	12

ABOUT THE AUTHOR

Stephen leVine was born in London and educated in Hove and London. After many years of travelling around the world working for a holiday tour company, he returned to England. In the 1970s, he started his own business in retail in Swindon, Wiltshire. He moved in 1985 to Hailsham, Sussex and became a resident of Eastbourne in 1987. With a keen interest in the history of Sussex, this is his third book.

By the same author:

Lords to Bureaucrats
A History of Sussex Town Halls and their local benefactors.

ISBN:-13: 978-0993544101   ISBN:-10: 099354410X
2016

A Napoleonic Defence
Hailsham Barracks 1803 – 1815

ISBN:-13: 098-0-9935441-2-5   ISBN:- 099354412X
2019

****

Printed in Great Britain
by Amazon